THE
Archive Photographs
SERIES

HARROGATE

Malcolm Neesam

The Royal Pump Room of 1842.

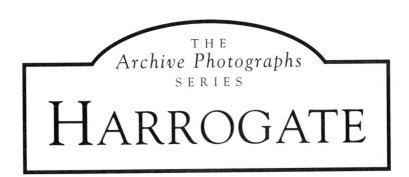

THE
Archive Photographs
SERIES

HARROGATE

Compiled by
Malcolm Neesam

CHALFORD

The Chalford Publishing Company
St Mary's Mill, Chalford,
Stroud, Gloucestershire, GL6 8NX

ISBN 0 7524 0154 8

Typesetting and origination by
The Chalford Publishing Company
Printed in Great Britain by
Redwood Books, Trowbridge

The Sulphur Well Temple of 1807–8.

Contents

Dedicated to my dear sister, Shirley

Introduction

The photographs reproduced on the following pages have been selected by the author for the purpose of giving the reader something of the flavour of old Harrogate. They have been assembled to either depict important aspects of the town's history or because they are attractive compositions in their own right. The rise of Harrogate as a place of popular resort occurred at the time of corresponding popularity for photography. Consequently, the town has been well recorded on film. Much, it is true, has been lost, such as the record of celebrations which accompanied the opening of the Victoria Park Estate, or the end of the Crimean War, and even such great public events as the opening of the Victoria Baths. Nevertheless, much remains. The author has arranged the photographs in broad subject groups which it is hoped possess a certain sequential logic. Thus the Spa, which transformed Harrogate from an obscure village in the Royal Forest, into 'the World's Greatest Spa', is the first group, followed by the Stray, which has been such an important adjunct to the Spa, and a framework around which the town developed. Then come Street Scenes, Transport, Hotels, Shops, Town's Business, Parks and Gardens, Entertainment, Spa Rooms & Kursaal, Church & Faith, Education, Celebrations, War, and Sport.

Harrogate in archive photographs depicts primarily the Harrogate of the nineteenth and twentieth centuries, and although the captions contain many references to earlier times, the emphasis has been placed on the rapid growth of the community which followed the great Award of 1778.

The history of Harrogate may for convenience be divided into six eras. First, there is the era of which we know least – that time when the land between the Anglo-Norse Harlow Hill and the River Nidd became settled, up to the earliest surviving documentary evidence for the existence of Harrogate in the Court Roll of 1332. Secondly, there is the era of Medieval Harrogate, with its Chantry Chapel, its forest law, and its plagues. The discovery in 1571 by William Slingsby of the Tewit Well opens the third era, which is closed in 1778 when the great Award protects the Wells, establishes the Stray, and creates a framework for the future growth of the town. The fourth era is the time of Georgian and Regency Spa, when the Stray frontages are developed, the Theatre built, a racecourse provided, and public amenities constructed by the township – amenities such as the Assembly Rooms, the Sulphur Well Temple, and the Workhouse. The fourth era was also the time when community spirit had developed to such an extent that the prosecution of Thackwray was possible over the matter of the attempt to divert the public Sulphur Well. The 1841 Harrogate Improvement Act which followed the

Thackwray case marked the beginning of the fifth era, known as the time of the Improvement Commissioners. Great strides in local government reform occurred during the fifth era, despite strident opposition. The town was paved, sewered, watered, and lit. Modern policing was introduced. The railway arrived, bringing opportunities for the importation of vastly increased number of visitors, as well as building materials to satisfy the seemingly insatiable demands of builders such as Dawson, Ellis, and the Carter brothers. The Improvement Commissioners built the Royal Pump Room, protected the other Wells of the town, and eventually provided the New Victoria Baths and Market Buildings. The fifth era was also the hey-day of the Victoria Park Company, which linked the two ancient villages of High and Low Harrogate into a single town, providing it with the splendid streets which are so appreciated by modern residents and visitors. The very success of this fifth era ushered in the sixth, when in 1884 Harrogate began its life as a fully fledged municipality, with a Mayor, electoral warding, and the power to levy and spend rates for the benefit of the whole community. Never has Harrogate had so many capable citizens working for its advancement than as at the beginning of the sixth era – George Dawson, John Barber, the Carter brothers, the Simpsons, Richard Ellis, Sampson Fox, Charles Fortune – visionaries to the man. Under their leadership, Harrogate received the Royal Baths, the Kursaal, improvements to the Pump Rooms, a gigantic series of reservoirs and filter beds, the start of a Municipal Palace which included a monumental library. The private sector was encouraged to build the Duchy, West End Park, Dragon and Franklin estates. Two enormous luxury hotels, the Grand and the Majestic, were built, as was the Grand Opera House. The Valley Gardens were laid out, and the town acquired the Stray. Although some may believe that the sixth era came to an end in the catastrophe of 1914, or possibly in 1969 when the Royal Baths closed, or even in 1974 with local government reorganization, it is the author's belief that Harrogate is still in its sixth era, and that future historians will confirm that those events, policies, and values which are current at the time of writing were the direct outcome of the Charter of Incorporation of 1884.

Malcolm G. Neesam
Manor Place, April 1995

One

Spa

The first public baths to be erected in Low Harrogate were the Victoria Baths, built by an enterprising local business man, John Williams. He understood that the growing demand from visitors for Spa treatment could be satisfied only by a specially built amenity. Up to the turn of the eighteenth century, it had been High Harrogate's Chalybeate, or Iron, Waters which had been in greatest demand, but when the fashion for Sulphur Water developed c. 1800, Low Harrogate came into its own. Williams commissioned the Leeds architect John Clarke, who designed a single storey structure in an elegant exercise in Greek Ionic style. With its thirteen bathing suites and central reception hall, faced with an aristocratic range of columns and battered windows, the Victoria Baths of 1832 set a fashion for classical architecture which affected profoundly the future appearance of Harrogate. This photograph of 1874 shows the Victoria Baths at right; at left may also be seen the 1871 building of the New Victoria Baths, which was converted in 1930 into the present Municipal Buildings.

Joseph Thackwray, owner of the Crown Hotel, built the Montpellier Baths in the Crown Gardens in 1834, using an austere classical design by the York architect Andrews. At this time, the Crown gardens extended to Parliament Street, and their importance grew after the discovery of a series of mineral wells after 1822. The whole estate passed in 1869 to George Dawson, who – quite typically – started a series of major improvements which included the construction of a new pump room and a band stand – seen here at right. The original Montpellier Baths were described in a guide book of 1840 as being 'ornamented by a handsome portico. The entrance hall is lofty, and lighted with a dome. On each side of it there is a spacious waiting room – that on the right for ladies, the left for gentlemen. There are also shower baths, a hot air bath and a vapour bath.' The site was re-developed in the 1890's when the Royal Baths were built.

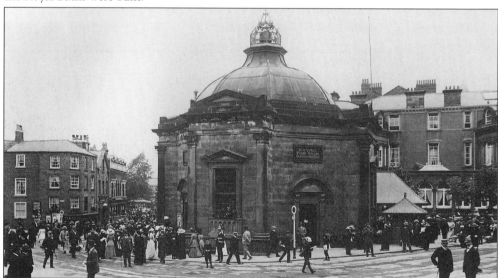

The Royal Pump Room covers the strongest known Sulphur Well in the World, which probably came into use for medical purposes in the early seventeenth century. It is mentioned in Edmund Deane's *Spadacrene Anglica*, published in 1626, and Celia Fiennes recorded that when in Harrogate for her tour of 1679–8, 'the small being so very strong and offensive that I could not force my horse near the well'. The present building was designed by Isaac Thomas Shutt and built in 1841–2. An outside pump was provided to ensure that the public's right of access to a free supply of sulphur water would be maintained. Here, we see early morning drinkers in the traffic-free zone around the Pump Room during the season of 1911.

The Royal Pump Room in 1897, decorated for the Diamond Jubilee of Queen Victoria. A controversy was raging at this time concerning the vexed matter of crowding at the Royal Pump Room. Some believed that a solution would be to demolish the 1842 building and replace it with a huge new structure in an inflated neo-Baroque style. Eventually it was decided to build a light-weight iron and glass structure, which would protect the springs.

The Royal Baths were opened on 3 July 1897 after being completed from plans drawn up by Baggalley and Bristowe of London for the national competition announced by Harrogate Council. This building, opened by HRH The Duke of Cambridge, soon came to be known as the most advanced centre for hydrotherapy in the world, offering a comprehensive range of treatment, under medical supervision. Architecturally, the Royal Baths is a triumph, as it manages to resolve that most challenging problem of constructing an imposing building at the foot of a steep hill, virtually on a single storey, and in such a manner as to combine the very different functions of treatment rooms, administrative areas, entertainment and leisure facilities, and council-run water bottling operations. The heart of the building is in the great pump room with its soaring dome, from which the other amenities are reached by means of axial corridors. If the overall influence is the Italian Renaissance, the effect is pure Victorian spectacle. The building presents an especially dramatic appearance when floodlit.

Contemporary visitors to the cooling rooms of the Turkish Baths described their appearance as like something from the *Arabian Nights*. As with other departments of the Royal Baths, the Turkish Section was decorated to a standard of the utmost opulence, being fitted with tiling, woodwork, flooring and furniture of most lavish and costly description. Every surface glowed with colour from the inlaid tiling, ceiling stencil work, and precious antique carpets which lined each room. Lighting of a soft and delicate nature pierced the steamy atmosphere, creating an other-worldly effect. Beyond the clock-mounted grill may also be seen the deep plunge pool, and at the extreme right the entrance to the 'Hot Room'. Although Turkish Baths could be found in many resorts throughout the length and breadth of the nation, many of which were on a much bigger scale than those pictured here, it is true to record that none were as exclusive or luxurious as Harrogate's own.

The senior staff of the Royal Baths pose on the Wintergardens staircase for this photograph of c. 1910, including members of the orchestra, who also performed at other venues connected to the Spa. At the bottom centre sits the General Manager, Sir Henry Buckland, who would shortly take his leave to manage the Crystal Palace in London.

Overleaf, pages 14 and 15: These three exotic visitors are sampling the Harrogate Waters from the central servery in the Royal Baths, to which waters from all over Harrogate were piped. The Kissingen Well, located beneath the entrance ramp to the main entrance of the Royal Baths, was an especially popular drink with visitors, so much so that bottles of Kissingen Water were sent round the world from the Royal Baths bottling department. This photograph shows part of the magnificent inlaid floor of the central pump room of the Royal Baths, and the great mahogany counter of the servery, which was quite shamefully broken up by the Council in the late 1960's. When the Dustin Hoffman/Vanessa Redgrave film *Agatha* was shot here some years later, a facsimile counter had to be assembled from papier maché.

The Royal Bath Hospital, built by charitable subscription in close proximity to the mineral wells of the Bogs Field, and opened in 1824–5, afforded the sick poor of the United Kingdom access to the healing waters of Harrogate. The land was given by the Earl of Harewood, and donations from George IV and many others, enabled the project to proceed. All of the Harrogate Inns provided 'subscription books' into which visitors entered promises to pay a charitable donation, and the growth of the Royal Bath Hospital may quite fairly be described as a massive and triumphant expression of charitable goodwill and generosity. A further rebuilding occurred in 1889, thanks to additional generous bequests and donations, including contributions from Queen Victoria and Samson Fox. This photograph of c. 1889 shows the influence of the Scottish baronial style made popular by Queen Victoria's beloved Balmoral. The whole point of the Royal Bath Hospital was to provide a charitable amenity in Harrogate – not in Bradford, Leeds or York, which already had hospitals of their own. The closure of the Royal Bath Hospital in 1994 and the subsequent removal of its amenities to Leeds is regarded by this author as a terrible betrayal of past charitable generosity, and as part of a pernicious trend of 'centralization' which – unless it is stopped – will result in the loss to the town of all National Health services.

The interior of the Royal Bath Hospital, after the major rebuilding of 1888–9, had the character of a grand hotel or modern stately home, rather than an establishment of charitable origin for the relief of the sick poor – but perhaps this says something of the nature and scope of Victorian philanthropy!

The Mineral Wells of Harlow Car are in all probability the subject of Dr. Short's reference to 'several ouzing springs in a marshy clay ground below Harrogate, of a saltish taste' which appears in his 1734 book on Mineral Waters. Since Dr. Short's time, the number of Mineral Springs at Harlow Car has increased to seven, of mild, alkaline sulphur, and a single chalybeate water. The picturesque setting of these wells led the owner of the estate to erect an Hotel and Suite of Baths in 1844, in a chaste Gothic style of architecture. Both buildings survive, the former as the popular 'Harrogate Arms Hotel', and the latter as offices for the Northern Horticultural Society. In this view of c. 1914 – the same year that Harrogate Corporation purchased this estate – visitors sample the delicious waters.

Harrogate's least known Spa building, the Peat and Plombieres Baths, is also the town's only example of Edwardian Spa architecture. It was built behind the Wintergardens from 1909–1911, largely at the recommendation of King Edward VII's physician Sir Frederic Treves, better known today for his role in the 'Elephant man' case. The utilitarian wings containing the baths were demolished in 1954 to make way for the Lounge Hall car park, but the exquisite waiting room survives, with its beautifully vaulted ceiling, elaborate plaster cornices, elegant columns, stained glass, and the finest wooden doorcase in Harrogate.

Localised electric peat baths were prescribed at the Royal Baths for patients with muscular and rheumatoid disorders. Sometimes called 'Schnee baths', the treatment consisted of encasing affected limbs in warmed peat through which electric currents were then passed.

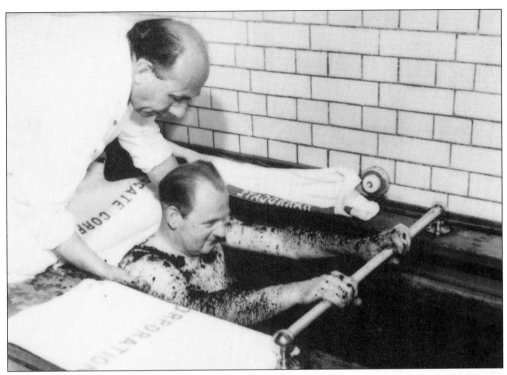

The Harrogate peat bath was a deeply relaxing therapeutic experience and was highly popular with visitors. Such baths were always provided under expert supervision.

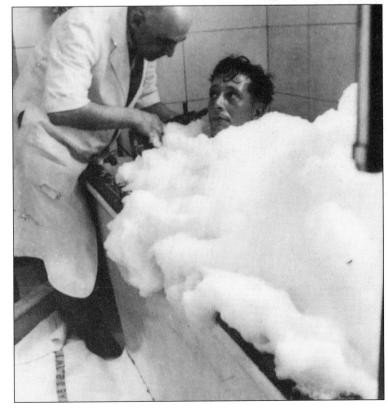

... As were the foam baths, which – when injected with extract of *pinus sylvestris* – surrounded the bather with an exhilarating cloud of pine essence.

An elaborate system of pipes and pumps enabled waters from all over Harrogate to be served in the great Pump Room of the Royal Baths. The mineral waters came from as far away as Oakdale, Starbeck, Harlow Hill and Valley Gardens, as well as from the many wells beneath the Royal Baths. No other Spa on Earth could offer its visitors so great a range of natural Mineral Waters as Harrogate, from the World's strongest Sulphur to the Pure Chalybeate, and all were available from this central counter.

The Royal Baths continued to function as a Spa throughout the difficult days of World War Two.

Harrogate corporation observed the most stringent standards for the testing and analysis of the Spa's Mineral Waters, which process was in the charge of Arnold Woodmansey, Borough Analyst, seen here in his office in Bath Terrace, overlooking the back of the Lounge Hall, *c.* 1940.

Overleaf, page 22: The only known photograph of Agatha Christie leaving the Old Swan Hotel after the missing novelist was identified in December 1926. The facts behind Miss Christie's disappearance are still vague, but many believe that a breakdown, induced by overwork, caused her to visit the Harrogate Spa after seeing an advertising poster at Waterloo Station in London. Fifty years on, the Dustin Hoffman/Vanessa Redgrave film *Agatha* was shot in Harrogate.

Two

Stray

The Stray owes its existence to a movement in the 1760's to sell the 'wastes' of the great Royal Forest of Knaresborough. At this time, all of the known Harrogate Mineral Wells were on land owned by the Duchy of Lancaster, to which the public had access. Consequently, the Wells were heavily used and were the means by which the local Innkeepers were able to ply a lucrative trade. The alarm produced by the proposal to sell and enclose the Royal Forest may therefore be appreciated. To allay the fears of the residents, the Duchy sent a team of Commissioners to survey the area, following the Enclosure Act of 1770. The result of the Commissioners' deliberations was the great Award of 1778, which set aside two hundred acres of land to link all the then known wells, and to provide land for the exercise which was deemed so essential a part of the 'cure'. At the heart of the Award was the principal that the Stray should ' … for ever hereafter remain open and unenclosed, and all persons whomsoever shall and may have free access at all times to the said springs, and be at liberty to use and drink the Waters there arising, and take the benefit thereof … '. These words should be impressed upon every Harrogate child.

The St. John's Well on the Stray at High Harrogate was discovered in 1631 by Dr. Stanhope, who wrote about it in his book *Cures without care*, published the following year. The situation of the new well was considered to be an improvement on that of the Tewit Well, as it was on a ground 'very firme, whereby it giveth advantage of faire dry walkes, wherein the other is very defective' and that it had 'an admixture of brimstone, besides the iron and vitriol, which I take to bee an aditament of worth and nobleness'. In 1786 the St. John Well was given the protection of a Pump Room, erected at the expense of Lord Loughborough, whose Harrogate Mansion lay across the Stray a few hundred yards to the south. This building was in turn remodelled by the Harrogate Improvement Commissioners in 1842 who commissioned the architect of the Royal Pump Room in Low Harrogate, Isaac Thomas Shutt, to do the work. This photograph of the St. John's Well Pump Room dates from the 1880's, and has the caption 'Grandpa going hunting'.

Certain parts of the Stray have always been popular points of assembly, either because of proximity to a Mineral Well or place of entertainment. The so-called 'Pier Head' at the top of Montpellier Hill was an ideal site for the bath chairs which were such a feature of the late Victorian Spa. A speedier form of transportation was also available in the form of the donkeys which may be seen at right. St. Peter's Church in the background was at this time (*c.* 1890) without its tower.

The first serious attempt to beautify the fringes of the Stray began in 1860 when the Improvement Commissioners undertook a programme of tree planting. The rough state of the roads and footpaths may be seen in this contemporary photograph. At left, the White Hart, which had been rebuilt in 1846, followed by Royal Parade which was developed during the same decade. At centre, the Royal Pump Room of 1842, to the right of which stands the Crown Hotel with its rebuilt central portion of 1847. George Dawson's Montpellier Parade may be seen at far right, still in the course of construction. The small stone well-head on the Stray housed a pump for the St. Anne's Well, the water from which was recorded by historian William Grainge as making the best tea in Harrogate.

Until George Dawson began his building activities in the 1860's, in Low Harrogate, the best buildings which fronted the Stray were generally in Georgian High Harrogate. This imposing terrace may pass as Georgian, until the observer notices the spiked dormer windows, and the two wooden bays at each end, which betray the Victorian origins of the building. Situated critically between Christ Church and the Georgian Theatre, this terrace dominates the view of Church Square from the north Stray. Its subtle proportions have unfortunately been ruined by the loss of the elegant iron railings and demolition of all three ionic porticos. The restoration of these features should be a priority for any programme of enhancement for High Harrogate, which in truth is still an underrated jewel in Harrogate's crown.

Some twenty years after their planting in the early 1860's, these saplings on Montpellier Hill have developed into a definite boundary for the Stray. In order to enable the Stray's herbage to be kept under control, the Stray Acts had created imaginary 'gates' which were allotted to local land owners. Each 'gate' entitled the owner to depasture a prescribed number of beasts on the Stray. This view of c. 1885 shows cows grazing on Montpellier Stray. Harrogate Corporation bought out the gate holders in 1893, the new Stray Act requiring them to pay £230 per gate in compensation.

Harrogate was given its Stray by the Duchy of Lancaster, whose commissioners were responsible for the great Award of 1778 which set aside two hundred acres of the Royal Forest as a public space. The public right of access to all parts of the Stray is guaranteed by the Acts of Parliament. Thanks to the foresight of its officers, the Duchy retained the freehold of the Stray, which has enabled it to veto any plans for fashionable construction projects, and therefore ensure that the sanctity of the stray remains unviolated. As well as this interest, the Duchy received some of the land which fronted the Stray, through the award of 1778. This land was subsequently developed by the Duchy who went to extreme lengths to ensure that Harrogate received buildings of the very highest architectural standards. The five mansions fronting the Stray between Knaresborough Road and Wetherby Road were typical Duchy developments. Alas – all five mansions were swept away after 1960 to provide land for a new District Hospital, the buildings of which now present an utterly mediocre Stray-side frontage.

Later generations often forgot that the 'Bogs Field' in Valley Gardens had always been part of the Stray, and an especially important part due to the existence of several significant mineral wells in the vicinity. Direct access to Bogs Field – so called because the overflowing wells turned the surface into a bog – was not by the footpath along by the stream, but by Cornwall Road, which was itself designated part of the Stray under the great Award of 1778. The waters of Bogs Field were noted by Dr French in his 1652 publication *The Yorkshire Spa*. One of the wells proved to be especially popular in Victorian times – the Magnesia Well – and in order to provide it with an appropriate home, the Improvement Commissioners built a little Gothic pump room in 1858. The waters of Bogs Field were the main reason for the establishment of the Royal Bath Hospital in 1824 on the neighbouring site, donated by the Earl of Harewood. The hospital, opened for the reception of patients in 1825, may be seen in the right background of the photograph, which dates from *c.* 1880.

In the early years of the twentieth century, the detached portion of Stray at Well Hill was provided with posts and chains to prevent wheeled vehicles from damaging the footpaths and grass. The Stray also ran from Ripon Road to the frontage of the Swan Inn, then known as the Harrogate Hydro, forming a pleasant green oasis to the right of the main entrance to the Inn. At the time of writing, this detached portion of Stray has been filtched by the rapacious motorist to deposit unsightly piles of scrap metal. Wake up, Harrogate!

A good general rule for the Council to observe in respect to the Stray is to leave it alone. Although the original Award of 1778 has been amended and superseded several times by such deeds as the Acts of 1789, 1841, 1893, 1985 & 1986 the concept of providing a public open space of some 200 acres which should be 'forever open and unenclosed' has survived unscathed. However, in 1933 the Council ignored the protests of the townspeople and reduced considerably the area of the Stray by means of cutting a series of large flower beds into the turf at West Park. This act of 'gilding the lily' was resented fiercely, and massive opposition mounted. The Stray Defence Association came into being. Undaunted, the Council removed a further 5,000 square yards in May 1934 – but then came the elections which were contested by Stray Defence Candidates, who swept the unrepentant councillors from office. The Stray was restored after November 1934.

The winter of 1934–5, and council workmen remove the illegally planted shrubs and flowers from West Park Stray, after the biggest row experienced by the town during the twentieth century.

A lesser known, but equally important Stray battle took place in 1923 when the Council sanctioned the building of public lavatories on the Stray directly opposite the Prince of Wales Hotel. As this construction was within seventy five yards of the Prince of Wales (and remember, this was well before the Prince of Wales roundabout was laid out) the lavatories should have been built underground. A town's meeting compelled the council to cease their building work, and a number of public spirited individuals subscribed to the cost of obtaining an injunction to restore the Stray.

Three

Street Scenes

Starbeck Highstreet looking towards Forest Lane Head, photographed shortly before the First World War. The handsome terra cotta façade of the Star Inn is still intact at right, and the traditional gas lamps dating from the 1840's also carry their Prussian caps with bristling dignity. The Star Inn was rebuilt in 1904, and closed in the 1940's.

High Harrogate Stray at its narrowest point where the late-eighteenth-century Westmorland Street joins the very much older Devonshire Place. The Devonshire Inn is a building of some architectural significance, but the adjoining building to the right is not without interest, as its archway led to premises occupied by Pickersgill Palliser. Appointed as Harrogate's post master in 1837, Palliser had become the publisher and proprietor of the *Harrogate Advertiser* in the previous year.

Regent Parade at left and Devonshire Place at right betray their eighteenth-century origins in their names, although both grew from far more ancient roots in the old village of High Harrogate. The junction of Regent Parade with Westmorland Street, at the point where the Stray is at its narrowest, was transformed by the Stray Act of 1893, which for the first time permitted public lavatories to be erected on Stray land – always subject to the requirement that any such constructions occurring within 75 yards of an existing building must be placed underground. The dark 'hump' in the distance is the ornamental rockery which was placed on top of the recently built public lavatories. When the Council replaced the original lavatories in the 1950's, they built above ground, and thereby not only ruined the view across High Harrogate's most sensitive locality, but also flouted the Stray Act of 1893.

Oatlands Drive, at a time when it was known as Paley Lane, after the Paley family who built and occupied Oatlands House. The trees to the right of the road were planted at the behest of Alexander Wedderburn (Lord Loughborough) in the 1780's as part of the garden design for Wedderburn House, and it is probable that the cottages – which still stand – were originally built for the agricultural labourers on the Wedderburn estates. When the Act of 1789 sought to provide land in compensation for Stray lost through the construction of roads and footpaths, the verges of Oatlands Drive were added to the Stray as 'slips'.

The eastern end of James Street was designed by J.H. Hirst of Bristol as an Italianate terrace of red brick and stone facing, which featured a splendid stone colonnade running the length of the ground floor façade between Station Square and Princes Street. It was built at the behest of Richard Ellis, who wished to provide Harrogate with a new and imposing entrance from the recently opened central Railway Station. At left may be seen the great mass of the Station Hotel, designed by Arthur Hiscoe in 1873, and later completed round into Albert Street by architect Bown in 1890. All these buildings were executed to the highest standards of construction, the hotel in particular having some magnificent carved stone decoration. At extreme left may also be glimpsed the Victoria Park Methodist Church, built by architect J.H. Hirst in 1865, on land donated by Richard Ellis, who subsequently provided several further generous bequests. The curious object beneath the lamp post was one of the water fountains provided for the refreshment of pedestrians.

James Street *c*. 1870, with Vine Villa, the Victoria Hall, and Prospect Hotel. Vine Villa stood at the junction with Princes Street, and was built in 1860 by architect J.H. Hirst for the Carter family, of whom Nicholas Carter later became the first Mayor of Harrogate. In 1883 plans were laid by the Bradford Old Bank to construct a branch on the site of Vine Villa. This bank was itself demolished in 1938 for the present building of Barclays Bank. The Victoria Hall was erected on its James Street site *c*. 1832, being formed from the dismantled Chapel of St. John from High Harrogate. The Hall provided a home for the Mechanics Institute, one of whose chief supporters was Richard Ellis. In the distance, the Prospect Hotel forms the last building on the south side of James Street.

James Street, for long regarded by many as the town's premier shopping street, was paved across with wooden blocks to keep down the sound of passing traffic – especially the horse-drawn variety! Long before James Street existed, however, High Harrogate's Regent and Devonshire Parades were attracting the visitors with their superb range of 'London Fashions'. When Low Harrogate sprang into fashion in the very early nineteenth century, the footpath between Prospect Hill and Paradise Row (as Park Parade was then known) became well used. Following the purchase of a large part of central Harrogate by James Franklin in 1810, the western half of the footpath began to assume the characteristics of a shopping street, and the landlord's Christian name was applied to it. This picture dates from *c*. 1912, and includes at left the premises of Ogdens and Marshal and Snelgrove.

At the time of writing, this Station Parade site is occupied by Safeways food store which was built when the old Spa Garage was demolished in the 1980's. The right of this photograph shows the Spa Garage in the course of erection in the grounds of the substantial Gothic villa which bears all the hallmarks of Arthur Bown's work for the Victoria Park Company. Station Parade was, after Victoria Avenue, the Victoria Park Company's most important development, and was lined with a series of splendid detached mansions, most of which have subsequently been swallowed up by development on the Safeways' site. The elaborate 'figure of eight' railings were used widely across the Victoria Park Company's estate, but few now remain due to the salvage programme of the Second World War.

Cheltenham Parade, which today is a traffic-choked thoroughfare of interesting private shops and businesses, began its life as part of the Victoria Park Company's northernmost residential development. It was the last link between Station Parade and the ancient Baker Lane (later Walker Road and finally King's Road) which connected Low Harrogate to Bilton, being developed only after 1870. These were comfortable, substantial houses for the middle classes, and many of them were used as lodgings by visitors to the Spa. The provision of trees was an essential aspect of Victorian residential design in Harrogate, and this view shows the recently planted saplings and their protective guards.

The view from West Park, northwards, along Parliament Street and Ripon Road, taken *c.* 1927, showing at right the newly erected War Memorial. Following the conversion of many of the houses into hotels, the gardens were integrated until they became a single open feature which by mutual consent was maintained by the Council. At the centre of the picture rises the Café Imperial, which fifty years later would be occupied by Betty's.

The southern end of Parliament Street received definitive form during the 1860's when George Dawson began building on a large scale. The straight terrace at right, with its projecting first floor 'pagoda' windows, was built by George Dawson from 1866–8. Half way through this work, Dawson began to build the much bigger Cambridge Crescent at right, which carried Parliament Street so effectively into the newly developing town centre in Prospect Square. Cambridge Crescent was designed by J.H. Hirst, and was built between 1867–8. By *c.* 1926, traffic is already beginning to dominate the scene. Today, little has changed, save for the demands made by motorists, which have reached insane proportions.

This four-square, solid villa in Parliament Street, stood on the site of the Westminster arcade of 1898, which for many years was occupied by the premises of Charles Walker's furniture store. The villa shown here was the home of Harrogate's redoubtable Medical Officer of Health, Dr. Titus Deville.

Montpellier Parade between Montpellier Gardens and Montpellier Street was built by George Dawson in the early 1860's and played an important role in schemes to link up the two ancient villages of High and Low Harrogate. The architect is unknown, but it is not unlikely that Dawson himself prepared the plans, which incorporated Ashfield House, where the Thackwray family had provided lodgings for particularly important visitors to the Crown Hotel. The terrace terminated at the Montpellier Hotel, and this view includes Salbert's, the 'reliable and exclusive furrier' next to which were the premises of Madame Louis, the Jeweller and Tortoiseshell specialist, Crosby's the dispensing and analytical chemists, Basil Lodge the Tailor, and Megson the Fine Art and Antique dealer. It is interesting to note that although the picture clearly dates from c. 1914, the post card on which it is reproduced is dated 20 February 1945, and has an incorrect caption.

The junction of Cold Bath Road with the Esplanade formed part of land which stretched as far as Otley Road, and which the great Award of 1778 had allotted to the King. Work began on the development of Harrogate's first 'Duchy' estate in the 1850's, with the construction of the splendid villas of Beech Lodge and Beech Villa, but the state of the junction with Cold Bath Road remained dilapidated for many years. The reason for this was that the land was tenanted by an elderly man – one Harper by name – who sub-let to several under-tenants and whom the Duchy of Lancaster were loath to turn out. When Harper died, the Duchy were able to effect improvements. Cold Bath Road itself is of very ancient origin, taking its name from the Cold Well which was used to treat eye conditions, as well as for bathing.

Well Hill developed round the old Sulphur Well after 1600, largely to provide accommodation for visitors and their landlords, in much the same way that High Harrogate grew up round the St. John's Well. This photograph shows, at left, Benwell House and its two neighbours, which were acquired by the corporation in the early 1920's, and subsequently demolished to extend the Valley Gardens. Cornwall House, at right, a beautiful Georgian property, was a popular resort with visitors who did not wish to stay at the larger inns such as the Crown or Swan. When Benwell House was demolished in the late 1920's, a spring was discovered which promptly became the eighty-ninth on the list of official Harrogate Wells.

The Ripon turnpike road was developed as a result of the Act of 1751, and greatly improved transportation between Ripon and Leeds. At the point where the Harrogate section of the turnpike road passed nearest to the old Sulphur Well, a number of developments were encouraged, including the George Inn and adjoining roads. This photograph of *c.* 1928 was taken a few yards north of the site of the old Turnpike bar, and shows the extreme width of the pavements, which have subsequently been sacrificed to the rapacious demands of the motor car.

Ash Grove, now part of King's Road, was a speculative development which was built partly with an eye for the demand for property which could be used to accommodate visitors. The area was by 1890 considered one of the most peaceful parts of Harrogate, as it faced the wooded extremity of the gardens behind the Spa Rooms, where the Conference Centre would later be erected. The road was not properly made up until 1911, when the works were paid for by Mr. W. Baxter of Knapping Mount, the inventor of the 'knapping' process of highway construction.

The centre of Low Harrogate, basking in the early sunshine of a quiet spring morning before the First World War. Taken from the roof of the Royal Baths, the view includes at far left a portion of the George Hotel, faced by a detached portion of the Stray, with the great bulk of the Hotel Majestic on the horizon, with its famous conservatory, known at the time as the biggest in the north. At centre stands the Kursaal, which is joined to the classical magnificence of the Spa Rooms by means of the crystal colonnade which contained the heavily-bepalmed Kursaal Café. Carriages await the convenience of visitors to the Royal Baths. When this photograph was taken, Harrogate was not only the 'World's Greatest Spa', but also the premier resort of the foremost power on Earth.

Four
Transport

When the Act of 1751 led to improvements to the Harrogate to Knaresborough Road, a toll house was established at Forest Lane Head. The turnpike road followed the route of the ancient 'Way to the hill of the soldier', or Heer-gate, from which Harrogate derives its name. These cottages still stand, though in considerably altered form.

The route of the old Brunswick railway line followed that of the modern Leeds-Harrogate line across the Crimple Valley viaduct and into Harrogate as far as Langcliffe Avenue, at which point it branched off to the north east towards the Brunswick Station. This photograph shows the entrance to the tunnel which traverses the length of Langcliffe Avenue. The line was opened for use in 1848, and closed in 1862 following the completion of the central Harrogate Railway Station.

An early photograph of the main platform of Harrogate Station, taken at some time during the 1870's. The white-banded chimneys of red brick were for little over a century a characteristic statement on the skyline of Station Square, as were the two water towers, one of which may be discerned at the right of this faded view.

The book stall at Harrogate Station, photographed in 1882, contained a goodly range of two- and three-volume novels then so popular with the travelling public. The posters tell of decisive British victories across the globe, and a notice at left advises that the 'London papers will arrive at 11.05am'.

Station Square is seen here in the spring of 1962. The old central Railway Station, at left, was built in 1862 to provide a much-needed link for the two lines which ended at Starbeck and the Brunswick. The provision of this central link meant that the development of central Harrogate could proceed apace, thanks to the sudden availability of the means for moving large supplies of building materials to the near-empty land in the vicinity. It was no coincidence that the opening of this central station was followed almost immediately by the building activities of George Dawson. One of the most attractive features of the old Station was its delicate canopy of iron and glass, which actually dates from c. 1890. For all its compact and discreet appearance, this Station dealt with an average of 100 trains a day in 1910, which is vastly more than arrive in the vile replacement structure of 1964–5.

Important visitors arriving at Harrogate Station could expect a lavish reception, with the laying out of the red carpet, and the provision of hundreds of elaborate floral decorations. Harrogate was known as a 'Silk Hat Station' because its importance ensured that the Station Master was given the rare privilege of being the bearer of a silk Top Hat!

The appearance of the first motor cars in Harrogate occurred on 9 May 1900, when the motor trial came to town. In this photograph, citizens inspect the vehicles parked outside the New Victoria Baths in Crescent Gardens – which later became the Municipal Buildings. An even greater stir was occasioned on the same day inside the building, where an inquiry by the Local Government Board took place. This looked into the borrowing by Harrogate Corporation of the immense sum of £35,000 for the waterworks undertaking. Fifteen days later, Harrogate celebrated the Relief of Mafeking.

The three great attributes of a world-class health resort – ample supplies of rich mineral water, attractive open spaces for exercise, and wonderfully pure country air – were possessed by Harrogate in great abundance. The last of these attributes has been poisoned most insidiously since 1900, when the first motor car trundled through the streets of the town. In this photograph, one of the entrants drives past Pier Head, having just passed the buildings for the Café Ophir (now Betty's), then in the course of construction.

Leeds Road on a fine summer's morning, shortly before the First World War. At right may be seen the great stone gate posts which lead to Royal Crescent. At left the junction with Tewit Well Avenue is being crossed by three citizens, who would doubtless have been astounded to learn that their descendants would countenance the illegal loss of the Stray slips, the narrowing of the footpaths, and the poisoning of the air – all for the convenience of the motorized brigade.

The motor trials of 1911 passed through the streets of Harrogate to the accompaniment of brilliant sunshine. Here, crowds in front of the Kursaal and George Hotel watch the arriving motorists making their ways to the Hotel Majestic. The leading car was driven by the Kaiser's brother, Prince Henry of Prussia. A leading opponent of the motoring fad at this time was Alderman Charles Fortune, who from his position on the Bench imposed stiff fines on individuals caught speeding at the 'disgraceful speed of ten miles per hour'. However, it has been recorded that the same august Alderman was, at an advanced age, to purchase a large motor car which the chauffeur was ordered to drive along Parliament Street, under no circumstances to exceed five miles per hour, and always on the crown of the road. Should this stately vehicle be met by another motorist, the chauffeur had orders to stand up and shout 'clear off!'.

Station Square, which developed almost accidentally, was improved in 1913 when the gardens were opened out and replanted, and new stone flags provided for the pavements. After the First World War, this little garden became so popular with nurse-maids and their charges, that it gained the nickname of Titty-bottle park!

A bus from the Pateley Bridge and Harrogate service, photographed shortly after the First World War at a Victoria Avenue Circus which was then in possession of its splendid iron railings. Victoria Circus was a pleasant green oasis dedicated for the use of residents of the Victoria Park estate who had keys for the entrance gates. There were seats, flower beds, a little tennis court, and a band stand, built in 1895, where Sidney Jones performed music on fine summer evenings for the delectation of the residents.

The junction of Leeds Road with Follifoot Lane as viewed from Spacey Houses at some time in the early 1920's. At left may be seen the Spacey Houses Hotel before its most recent rebuilding, and at right one of the several garages which mushroomed after the First World War. The Leeds-Harrogate road was greatly improved by a Parliamentary Act, which established the Turnpike, much of which was built by 'Blind Jack', the famous Yorkshire road builder. On the distant horizon the Crimple Valley railway viaduct may just be glimpsed.

In 1911, Lord Northcliffe, millionaire owner of the *Daily Mail*, organized the first round Britain air race, which boasted a phenomenal prize of £10,000, a sum which by the end of the century would be worth £2,000,000! Seventeen entrants took off from Brooklands at 4.00pm on 22 July, and eventually reached Hendon, after two had been required to drop out. The next section of the flight was the toughest, as the destination was Harrogate, at a distance of 182 miles. In the event, only six planes managed to touch down on the green expanse of Harrogate Stray between Oatlands Drive and Wetherby Road. It may be difficult in hindsight to anticipate the extent of the sensation caused by this event. Harrogate was agog. A huge grandstand with 450 yards of seating was erected, and spectators included the Mayor of Harrogate, Captain Boyd-Carpenter, Grand Duchess Xenia of Russia, Grand Duchess Ninon of Russia, the Lord Bishop of London, General Sir George Bullock, and the Under Secretary of State Sir William Byrne. A magnificent silver tea service had been acquired by the Harrogate Chamber of Trade to present to the winner, subject to the entirely reasonable reservation that the winner must be an Englishman. The first plane was sighted at a little after 7.00am, and the vast crowd held its collective breath – then the news was announced – Jules Vedrines, a FRENCHMAN!, the first to land after a flight of three hours, three minutes and four seconds. The second plane landed four minutes, 26 seconds later – the Chamber of Trade crossed its fingers – and the name of André Beaumont, a FRENCHMAN, was announced. Alderman Fortune commiserated with

the now nettled Chamber representatives: 'Shockin' bad form – these foreigners simply do not seem to know what's required of 'em'. Then came the third plane, 24 minutes and 58 seconds later – James Valentine – hurrah – an ENGLISHMAN. The band played patriotic music, the crowd cheered and waved Union Jacks, and amidst the congratulations of the bigwigs, Valentine received the silver service. It was, however, unfortunate that the weight of the service prevented Valentine's Deperdussin monoplane from taking off on the next stage of the race, so it had to be taken off by the Town Clerk, who took it home for safety and hid it under his bed.

It is not often understood by the citizens of Harrogate just how much Stray land has been lost during the years before the Second World War, the greater part of which was sacrificed for road widening programmes. This view from the upper floors of the Crown Hotel was taken in 1935 at the time of the laying out of the Crown Roundabout. Hitherto, traffic needs had been met by the centuries old crossing of Irongate Bridge and Cold Bath Road, but in 1935 a new roundabout was carved from the Stray. It is the knowledge of past losses – many of them in flagrant breach of the Acts of Parliament – which makes modern defenders of the Stray so sensitive with regard to further reductions.

Five
Hotels

THE GRANBY HOTEL,
HARROGATE

ENTRANCE AN
WEST WING.

The Granby Hotel is, at the time of writing, the oldest surviving hotel business in Harrogate. It is known to have existed in the late seventeenth century, when it bore the name of the Sinking Ship – an extremely old name which had its origins in the sinking of the Spanish Armada in 1588. In later times, the Inn became the Royal Oak, before assuming its present name of Granby in 1795, in honour of the Marquis of Granby, who won fame in the Seven Years' War. During the eighteenth and nineteenth centuries, the Granby was considered to be one of the foremost inns in England, and was Harrogate's most prestigious address. Clive of India was one of the many famous patrons to lodge at the Granby. In 1994–5 the Granby underwent a series of alterations to restore and enhance its fabric, with the east wing being converted into office accommodation.

The present Empress Hotel in Church Square, High Harrogate, has undergone a series of transformations since its establishment, the date of which is uncertain. Inquests of the Court of the Forest of Knaresborough were held here in the eighteenth century, and the oldest photographs of *c.* 1860 reveal a primitive single-storey structure with a white-washed frontage, known by the name of the Bay Horse. Later in the nineteenth century the establishment was rebuilt and given the more dignified name of the Empress, after which it became popular with the 'Commercial classes' as the *Advertiser* delicately put it! The decline of High Harrogate as a resort for visitors, in the years following 1870, led to the closure of several hotels. In the 1960's the Empress was again remodelled, with the second and attic storeys being removed, and the frontage drastically simplified to harmonize with the elegant Georgian building of Mansfield House, part of which may be seen on the extreme right of this photograph.

A wedding party, *c.* 1890, posing for the photographer Midgley Asquith outside the Empress hotel. Asquith was one of Victorian Harrogate's most successful professional photographers, whose studios were at Royal Parade.

The earliest known reference to an Hotel at the junction of the Harrogate-Leeds turnpike road with the ancient 'Way to the Hill of the Soldier' occurs in an advertisement placed by Michael Hattersley in the *York Herald* for 29 April 1815: 'Hotel, High Harrogate. Michael Hattersley (many years waiter at the Granby Inn) begs leave to inform the nobility and gentry that he has opened an Hotel at the cross-roads between High and Low Harrogate, which he has fitted up in a handsome and commodious manner; and respectfully solicits the honour of their patronage ... n.b. – Sulphur Water brought from the Wells every morning.' The Lake poets and their families stayed at Hattersley's in June 1827, which changed its name to the Royal 'Brunswick' in 1830. Eighteen years later, the new Harrogate railway station also adopted this name when it opened across the turnpike road to the south-east. This very old photograph, taken from the site of the Brunswick railway station, shows the first sight which would have greeted passengers alighting at Harrogate between 1848 and 1862, when the station closed. A tree-less York Place Stray is at extreme right.

Along with its northerly neighbour Brunswick Terrace, the Clarendon Hotel was the most important Georgian building on West Park It tripartite facade consisted of a plain central section, flanked by sections with fine bay windows. The Clarendon 'Victorianised' its ground floor at some point in the second half of the nineteenth century inserting ponderous angled bay windows as replacement for the elegant Georgian bows. The southern two-thirds of the Clarendon building were demolished in 1972 to make way for a loathsome prefabricated bellows-style structure.

The former Commercial hotel, later to be known as the 'West Park', probably grew from a humble 'beer house' which developed as West Park grew in importance. This photograph of *c.* 1880 was taken when the Hotel served as a headquarters for the Bicycle Touring Club. The magnificent decorative iron canopy and cornice cresting was removed during the salvage drive of *c.* 1940.

The Prospect Hotel, re-named as the Imperial Hotel in 1988, was built originally in 1814 by Nicholas Carter Senior as a private house. During the 'Season', the Carters took in visitors, the success of which led to the house becoming a regular hotel. The future first Mayor of Harrogate, 'young Nicholas' was born here. The Prospect was rebuilt in 1859 and 1865, but in 1870 further construction doubled its size. A new 82-foot tower was greatly admired, as it not only possessed a wealth of rich stone carving, but also provided the Harrogate skyline with an impressive addition. The Carter family remained in possession of the building until 1936, when it was sold to a Scarborough hotelier, who set about 'improving' the façade by removing most of the marvellous iron work.

The ancient thoroughfare of Cold Bath Road (once known as Robin Hood Lane) boasted several important hostelries in the great days of the Coaching era. One of the most interesting of these establishments was the hotel run by Mrs. Binns, who seems to have been one of the 'characters' of Georgian Harrogate. Binns' Hotel was doing sufficiently well by 1819 to enable it to contribute £14 13s towards the charity for the new Bath Hospital, a higher sum than any other collected by the town's hotels, save the Crown's £27 18s. By the time of Charles Dickens' visit in 1858, the hotel had adopted the more up-market name of 'Lancaster', in honour of the Duchy. Its fortunes declined, however, in the twentieth century, and for the last few years of its existence it served as a storage repository. Most of the building was demolished in the 1960's to make way for a characterless terrace of shops, although the section of the hotel which appears to the extreme right of the post card survives as a relic of the days when the great coaches rolled up to the Inn, and Charles Dickens was a guest.

The Wellington Hotel in Cold Bath Road may originally have been known as the Robin Hood Inn. It was built by John Harper in the early years of the nineteenth century, and had two sitting rooms and eight bedrooms. This photograph of c. 1870 shows the original Inn at left, which was a yellow-stucco structure with a typically elaborate door-case, and the Victorian extension at right with its stone frontage and bay windows. The Wellington was a coaching inn, but managed to survive the closing of the coaching service (which followed the arrival of the railways) by a substantial rebuilding programme to attract new guests. The building still stands in Cold Bath road, as a mixture of residential and commercial activity.

The White Hart was the most famous of all the inns of Cold Bath Road. With its ideal position at the junction of the Stray with Cold Bath Road, and within a stone's throw of the Sulphur Well, the White Hart was convenient for both travellers and health-seekers alike. The *York Courant* for 20 August 1765 carried an offer of fifteen shillings reward for the return of a dappled grey mare which had been 'Stray'd or conveyed from the White Hart in Low Harrogate.' The White Hart was one of the earliest Harrogate inns to be on the regular coaching runs, being the only Harrogate stop on the Fly between Carlisle and London in 1775. It was also the scene of the Waterloo celebrations on 9 September 1815, when the *Leeds Mercury* gave a report on 'the ball given by the Company at the White Hart … An unusual assemblage of beauty and fashion graced the rooms on that occasion, after partaking of an elegant supper'. This picture of the White Hart shows the building after its major reconstruction of 1847, when it was provided with a magnificent ashlar façade, which Professor Sir Niklaus Pevsner described as being the finest in Harrogate. The White Hart became a centre of the Health Authority's administration, after the Second World War.

The Crown Hotel, seen here from the Montpellier Gardens c. 1900, is perhaps the oldest of the Low Harrogate inns, dating in all probability from the end of the seventeenth century. The location of the Crown, a few yards from the world's strongest sulphur well, ensured that it was well-placed to serve the needs of the visitors who flocked to take the waters. In the eighteenth-century, the Crown came into the hands of the Thackwray family, under whom it prospered. When Lord Byron visited Harrogate in 1806, it was at the Crown that he stayed, although his visit was not without incident, as one of his dogs savaged a horse and had to be shot. Charges at this time were on the high side as a bed-chamber for a night, plus breakfast, lunch, dinner, tea, and supper cost 7/6, with an additional levy of 2s. on meals served in private rooms. The Crown was at the centre of the row of 1835–7, when its owner, Joseph Thackwray, was accused of trying to divert the waters of the public Sulphur Well onto the land of the Crown Hotel estate. At this time, the Crown's land reached as far west as Parliament Street. The central portion of the hotel was rebuilt in a massive and austere Palladian style in 1847, and the eastern and western wings followed after George Dawson purchased it in 1870. The Crown continues to this day to be one of Harrogate's great hotels.

The Crescent Inn probably came into existence during the middle years of the eighteenth century, when it was known as 'The Globe'. The earliest surviving account of a Harrogate Town Meeting took place at Thomas Linforth's the Globe Inn, on 28 October 1780, the same year which saw Sylas Neville visiting Harrogate and writing 'The Houses (i.e. Inns) here for the accommodation of the Company look more like gentlemen's seats than Inns, particularly the Globe Inn. ... ' Given the paltry appearance of the Inn even one hundred years later , it is likely that the writer confused the Globe with the Crown. A change of name followed, and the Globe became the 'Half-Moon'. By 1783 however, the name of 'Crescent' had been adopted. This was the year when a pair of new springs were discovered in the grounds of the Crescent, one of which – the Leamington Spring – became an important addition to Harrogate's range of medicinal waters. When the Crescent Inn was demolished at the end of the nineteenth century, it gave its name to the gardens which were created on the site.

Who today has heard of the Grosvenor Hotel, which stood in Crescent Road nearly opposite the ancient Crescent Inn? It had a very short life, but the splendid building it occupied survives as the location for a number of high quality business premises.

The Grand Hotel, designed by Christopher Brown of Hartlepool, was opened on 22 May 1903. Externally, its main contribution to the townscape was as an imposing backdrop to Valley Gardens, and a fanciful addition to Harrogate's skyline. The copper domes, which are now a pleasant weathered green, were originally covered in gold leaf so that they sparkled and shone like some oriental pleasure palace. Internally, the Grand was luxurious, with stained glass and

tapestries depicting scenes of old Harrogate. Here, we see the Palm Court, which also had a
resident group of musicians. The Grand was requisitioned during the Second World War and
re-opened in the early 1950's. After several sales the Grand ceased to be run as an hotel, and
converted to offices during the 1960's.

George Hotel from Parliament St. Harrogate.

The George Hotel – now known as the Swallow Hotel St. George – was established on Ripon Road at some point during the 1770's. This was an ideal location, being on the busy turnpike route between Ripon and Leeds, and within a couple of minutes' walk to the sulphur wells of Low Harrogate. In April 1828 the George Inn came into the hands of William Barber, whose family proceeded to run and enlarge it until the end of the nineteenth century. This photograph of *c.* 1905 shows the older 'Georgian' buildings of Ripon Road, and the large extensions erected between 1850–1896 which brought the frontage round into Crescent Gardens. The George Hotel has some of the best stained glass and plaster work in Harrogate, and maintains the town's Spa tradition by means of its excellent basement pool amenity.

The Hotel Majestic, from the time of its opening on 18 July 1900, established itself as a pre-eminent address for visitors to Harrogate. Designed by architect G.D. Martin, everything about the Majestic was on a magnificent scale. The interiors boasted the lavish use of costly materials, and the great 8,000 square foot conservatory was one of the largest in England. The Majestic rapidly became popular with the rich and famous, and was the scene for spectacular banquets during the glittering Edwardian era. Sir Edward Elgar described one of his visits to the Majestic in a letter to Alice Stuart Wortley dated 29 August 1912: 'Of course Harrogate thinks itself very fashionable & more than chic – & the ladies dress up terribly!'

Six

Shops

The West Park premises of Wilson and son, Chemists, as decorated for the coronation of Edward VII in 1902. At right may be seen a fragment of the fine Regency architecture of the Clarendon Hotel building, which has subsequently been spoiled through the addition of an intrusive plate glass window.

West Park has been a favoured location for ale houses, inns, and hotels since the development of the turnpike roads in the second half of the eighteenth century. The wine and spirit merchant H.O. Shutt, was a member of the family who developed the cottage community on York Place known as 'Shutt Hill', and who also owned the important Swan Inn at Low Harrogate. The vaults at left still operate as a popular pub. At right, the West Park branch of Goodrick, the family butchers, occupies the ground floor premises of the tall late Victorian building which dominates the area.

Prince's Street, photographed c. 1920, was home to the well-known fashion house of Croft, which closed in 1993. The Medici Gallery at right was a precursor of another highly reputable Harrogate business, Warners, Dealers in Antique Silver and Jewellery, which still provides customers with the highest standards of stock and service.

The name of Woods has been
synonymous with fine linen
since the eighteenth century,
when Castle Mills at
Knaresborough first produced
material for the family. The
present business was founded in
1895 at 7 Prince's Street by W.E.
Woods, the success of which led
to removal in 1926 to its present
premises on Prince Consort
Row. Woods is believed to be
the last speciality linen shop in
the United Kingdom, and is
celebrated nationally, both for
the wonderful quality of its
comprehensive stock, as well as
for its superb standard of service.
Here, the founder observes the
linen weaving process in Ireland.
Above may be seen Woods
Princes Street premises, c. 1920.

The little single-storey building, which today occupies the site at the corner of Beulah Street, Station Parade, and Cambridge Street, was formerly situated much further down Beulah Street to the north The construction of lower Beulah Street to an enlarged pattern before the First World War brought about the removal of Denton's business, who took their building with them! For some years, the re-erected building had a central public passage which warranted the description of 'arcade'.

A delivery of the world famous Harrogate toffee to premises in Station Parade, shortly before the 1914 war. Taylors the chemists had branches of their business at 2 Cambridge Crescent, 16 Beulah Street and 54 Station Parade, but their Station Parade shop closed in 1923 when John Pemberton's Billiard Rooms took over the lease. The elaborate 'Dutch gable' in the background was the entrance to an arcade which connected with the Central and Lowther arcades, and which thus provided the central shopping area with a network of covered walk-ways.

Batchelor's florist's shop in Station Square was a familiar sight to visitors as they emerged from Harrogate Railway Station. It opened in 1892 and closed a century later, still retaining the atmosphere and appearance of an old-fashioned establishment.

Edward Standing's café and grocery first opened its doors for business in 1882. The building contained a basement smokeroom, lined with oak panels, a ground floor grocery, an 'oriental' café on the first floor, and a second floor bakery. Much of the building's rich decorative features were lost after the First World War, when the stained glass panels were removed from the windows, and 'modern' signage introduced. This photograph was taken shortly after the post-war refurbishment, and the commissionaire may be seen to the left of the entrance. Standings closed in February 1982, to the lasting regret of its customers.

The James Street wing of Standing's, shortly before the post-War alterations of *c.* 1920 which removed the stained glass windows from the Oriental Café, and the beautiful Victorian signage from the fascia. At centre may be seen that portion of the building which was occupied by Baxter & Sons, 'Cigar and Cigarette Merchants'.

Standings Oriental Café, photographed shortly before the First World War. An atmosphere of 'mystery and invitation' was created by means of heavily inlaid Eastern furniture, a ceiling of Moorish vaults, stained glass windows, and cut glass gasoliers which produced a brilliant, sparkling light. Standing's Oriental Café was a popular centre of café life in Harrogate for nearly forty years, rivalled only by the Kursaal Café with its palms and famous clientele. However, shortly after the First World War the management decided upon a scheme of 'modernization' and the unique furnishings and decor were swept away for replacement by 1920's functionalism.

Joah Baxter established a tobacconists business in Royal Parade in 1868, but re-located to James Street in 1882, taking premises in the block built at the corner with station square for Edward Standing's grocery emporium. Much of Victorian window-dressing consisted of cramming as many items as possible into whatever space was available, as this photograph amply demonstrates.

One of the earliest businesses to open in Ellis's James Street development was Hodgson Smith, a stationer and fancy goods retailer. His business seems to have been established c. 1878 and ran until 1906. In that year, he retired, and the street directories for 1907–8 contain a new entry, '10 East Parade, Hodgson Smith Gentleman'. Here, Hodgson Smith poses outside his premises in the year of his retirement.

When Hodgson Smith retired from his Stationer's business at no. 1 James Street, he was succeeded by two new businesses, Randall's bootmakers, and Sim Hart the furrier and costumier. Sim Hart moved in 1907 followed by Randall's in 1908. Sim Hart was a very up-market business which considered that its image would be improved by ripping out the beautiful ground floor colonnade from Hirst's building, and treating the upper storeys with their delicate polychrome brick and stone decoration to a bland coat of white-wash. A grotesquely intrusive advertising sign was also erected. Sim Hart's business was an important part of commercial life in the James Street of the 1920's and 1930's, closing in *c*. 1938. It in turn was succeeded by the retailer of 'Women's Sportswear', Falkingham's.

Although greatly altered in appearance, this structure still stands in James Street at the corner of the passage which leads to Market Square. It was built originally in 1852 as the Salem Chapel for the United Methodists (who were then known as the Wesleyan Reformers) but with the rise of James Street as a commercial centre, it was sold in 1865 and converted into a fine arts repository called 'The Pantheon' under the ownership of Isaac Greenbury. Towards the end of the nineteenth century the building was again converted, into the 'King's Arcade', but in the twentieth century it spent much of its life as premises for a shoe shop.

The junction of Prince's Street and James' Street, shortly before the premises were occupied by the Yorkshire Penny Bank. The building formed part of the great terrace designed by Hirst which was developed by Richard Ellis, and its first occupant, in 1865, was the central Harrogate Post Office.

A photograph which often causes confusion! The mock-Tudor building at centre disappeared in the 1930's when Marshall and Snelgrove (at left) extended their premises as far as Walter Davey's photographic studio (at right). Marshall and Snelgrove had come to Harrogate in 1906, when they occupied premises at 38 James Street, and so great was their success that within five years they were obliged to build a larger store further along James Street. Number 38 was occupied by Ogdens 'Little Diamond shop' in 1910.

James Street, *c.* 1946, viewed from west to east. At left are the splendid Edwardian premises of Marshall & Snelgrove, the white tiled frontage of which introduced a new kind of commercial architecture to the streets of Harrogate. The impressive figure of Marshall and Snelgrove's Commissionaire may be seen on the pavement.

James Street celebrated the Armistice of 1918 with flags and patriotic devices. The Italianate stone-faced building at left was built in 1870 by George Dawson to a design by Hirst, and possessed magnificent ground floor frontages, which were subsequently destroyed by the shop-keepers. The last survivor is at centre, until it too succumbed to the English mania for replacing shop frontages every few years.

The chemists Wilson and son were one of the most respected businesses of old Harrogate. The firm's James Street premises were acquired in 1928 by Ogdens, as part of that firm's programme of enlargement.

Wilson and son ran a branch of their chemists shop from West Park, as well as James Street, the premises later being occupied by Trevvett Furnishers. The elaborate decorative iron work on the window was once a common sight in the town, although much has been lost through ignorance and indifference.

The illustrious firm of Ogden's was founded in 1893 by James R. Ogden, whose shop opened on 27 April at 23 Cambridge Street. J.R. Ogden was one of the most remarkable businessmen, who combined all the skills of a master jeweller and clock maker with a brilliant head for business. During the following years he opened and closed premises in Harrogate in order to be in the vanguard of commercial success, and eventually moved to 38 James Street, where he opened in 1911. The interior of Ogden's James Street premises has here been captured by an artist at some time during the Great War of 1914–18, and depicts some of the magnificent stock of silver and jewellery for which the business has always been famed. One hundred years after its foundation, the firm of Ogdens Ltd is unquestionably one of the top businesses in Harrogate, and one which still provides its customers with the quiet, discerning and expert service which was J.R. Ogden's own hallmark.

Wilford and Howard, General Drapers, occupied these well-favoured premises on George Dawson's cyclopean Prospect Crescent from 1882 to 1919, from which they supplied the gentry with blouses, corsets and underwear, and the Royal Baths with acres of huck-a-back towelling for use in the Turkish department. At right, a fragment of the flamboyant decorative iron work of the Prospect Hotel.

The West Riding Motor Volunteers Harrogate Squadron established itself in Salisbury Hotel Buildings, Albert Street, in 1918, but following the Armistice, became redundant. The enterprising E.R. Davies set up a motor repair business in their premises, which ran until 1922, when they transferred to 20 Station Parade. Here, the Albert Street shop is seen *c.* 1921 with a smartly dressed motorcyclist standing in the doorway.

This Cambridge Street property, photographed in 1928, was demolished in 1933 to make way for Marks and Spencer. The road through the centre of the block led to a garage owned by builder Amos Chippindale, which originally had been part of Belle Vue, a large house occupied in the 1820's by Captain Thrush, R.N. The building on the right still stands, as does St. Peter's Church at left.

Betty's Café, established in 1919, was located originally on Cambridge Crescent in the great curving terrace built from 1863–8 by George Dawson to a design by J.H. Hirst. In the mid-1970's Betty's moved across to the Scottish baronial building in Parliament Street which had been the home of the Café Imperial. That Betty's today is one of Harrogate's most successful and popular businesses is due to the astute management of its Board of Directors, who have responded to the public demand for a quality service. For the visitor who seeks the best that Harrogate café life has to offer, a visit to Betty's is essential. Here, the interior of Betty's may be seen as it appeared in the 1920s.

This property at the corner of Montpellier Square and Montpellier Parade was heightened with a mansard roof in the early years of the twentieth century at a time when this link between Low and Central Harrogate was becoming fashionable. The sole agents for the 'Imperial Boot', Joy Brothers, closed their doors many years ago, but the premises at right were occupied by the popular Harrogate caterer of Hammond Mann from c. 1933 to c. 1980.

The Victoria Park Company's residential development around Cheltenham Parade led to a demand for consumer products which encouraged traders to the western end of Chapel Street in the later years of the nineteenth century. The Argenta Meat company opened a butcher's shop on the ground floor premises of the former Methodist Chapel at the corner of Beulah Street and Chapel (now Oxford) Street. A side of beef in the window carries a sign proclaiming that the beast has been 'fed by the king'!

The building at the junction of Oxford Street and Commercial Street which later came to be occupied by a large draper's business, was for many years tenanted by the Stationers, Proctor Brothers, and Pork Butcher R. Simpson. Fred Proctor was one of the town's characters, as well as being a noted defender of the Stray, and a local historian. At the time of the 'battle of the flower beds' in 1933, Proctor assembled a good-natured crowd in front of his premises, distributed pea shooters, and marched on the Municipal Buildings to protest against the despoilation of the Stray.

This fishmonger, poulterer and fruiterer does not appear to have prospered in its Oxford Buildings location at the corner of Commercial Street and Oxford Street, as it is only listed in the directories between 1928 and 1930. The premises were taken over by Rose and Co. Wallpaper Merchants, in 1935.

Chapel Street, renamed Oxford Street in 1908, grew in commercial importance in the early years of the nineteenth century, especially after the opening in 1824 of the Methodist Chapel at the corner of Beulah Street. As a route, however, the street goes back well before the nineteenth century, as it served as the principal pathway between the Low Harrogate Sulphur Well and the chapel of St John's on High Harrogate Stray. Businesses such as Dickinson the Fruiterers relied on their custom from the neighbouring lodging houses of Parliament Street, as well from the passing trade brought by visitors.

All of these properties at the corner of Chapel (later Oxford) Street and Parliament Street were eventually incorporated into Buckley's store, now known as Debenhams store. The fishmonger at 36 Brayshaw (later Bentley's), was acquired as late as c. 1935, but Gibson the hairdresser at 38, and Wade the fruiterer at 40, were incorporated in 1909, promptly demolished, and replaced with a new wing of Buckley's. This wing set the pattern for future developments at Buckleys, being of red brick with stone facings.

The site at the corner of Oxford and Parliament Streets was long occupied by the Holroyd photographic studio. By the end of the nineteenth century Charles York, draper, was in business, but he was bought out by Buckley in 1900, his address being 22 Parliament Street. The success the firm enjoyed enabled it to acquire the ramshackled shop premises further up Oxford Street, which were replaced in 1909 by a large structure of red brick with stone facings. The new building was in an eclectic Dutch Baroque style, with Art Nouveau detail, and was accordingly a most unusual addition to the townscape. A few years later, the old Buckley's building at the corner of Parliament Street was rebuilt to match the Oxford Street section.

Buckley's store, opened in 1900 at 22 Parliament Street, went from strength to strength, and acquired 24 (Phillipson's Musical Instruments) in 1921, 26 (Tetley's Tobacconists) and 28 by 1940, and by 1950 it owned the whole site between Oxford Street and the Westminster Arcade consisting of Parliament Street 22–30. Parliament Street 26–30 were demolished in the 1950's to make way for a major rebuilding in a bland international anonymous style of architecture, out of keeping with the rest of Parliament Street.

Parliament Street, *c.* 1950, still with two-way traffic and wide pavements. At left may be seen one of the trees which grew on the unbuilt portion of the Royal Bath Estate, which was lost when the redevelopment programme of 1962 inflicted the concrete tower of Harrogate House on the locality. In the early years of the nineteenth century the bottom of Parliament Street had a bridge to carry traffic across the water course which ran down from the Cold Bath Road area and flowed into the grounds of the Spa Rooms estate.

Ripon House was built at the corner of the old Baker Lane and Parliament Street in the early years of the nineteenth century by John Oddy who also owned the field across the road on which important mineral springs were discovered in 1818. For many years, Ripon Houses provided lodgings for visitors, especially those who came for the Cheltenham waters. The central portion of the building was later tenanted by Oddy Wilson's, Jewellers.

The last of the purely residential properties between Cheltenham Parade and Parliament Street were converted to retail use in 1925. Union Street, at far left, was one of the very few areas of Harrogate which rated the modern term of 'deprived', the others being Tower Street and Smithy Hill. The main thoroughfare of King's Road received its name only in 1910 when W.H. Baxter paid for a number of improvements to the area, including the widening of the road which was known at the time as 'Walker Road'.

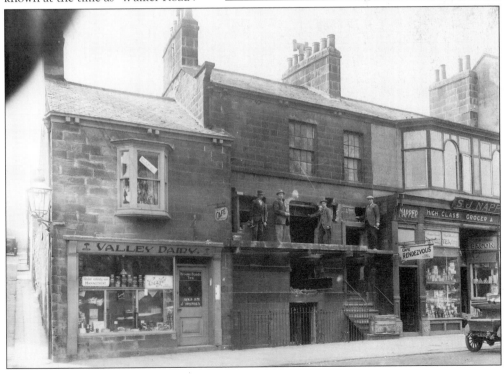

The Low Harrogate post office was ideally situated, being opposite the Royal Pump Room. The tenant, Horner, stands on the steps beneath a sign which advertises the Burial Board office for the parish of St. Mary. 'Public Library' refers to the private collection of books displayed on the premises from which paying customers could borrow.

ORIENTAL LOUNGE,
High-Harrogate.
A. FATTORINI,

RESPECTFULLY announces to the Visitors and Inhabitants of Harrogate, that he has on hand a large

STOCK OF JEWELLERY,

Sheffield Plated Goods and Berlin Silver, which he is enabled to offer at extremely low prices.

Also Ladies, and Gentlemen's Dressing Cases, Writing Desk, Work Boxes, Umbrellas, Parasols, and a variety of other articles.

Cut Glass Decanters,

Tumblers, and a variety of Table Lamps, &c. &c.

August 10th, 1837.

Harrogate is fortunate that despite the loss of many good private shops of character, the town is still home to several splendid businesses which have survived changing fads and fashions and continue to provide the very highest standards of stock and service. Of these, none have such a long and distinguished history as Fattorini's. Antonio Fattorini was born in Italy in 1797 and came to England to escape the unsettling times of the Napoleonic Wars. Antonio and his wife moved to Harrogate in 1831 and took premises at 14 Regent Parade – a splendid Georgian building at the heart of Regency Harrogate. Their shop, the 'Oriental Lounge', opened during the exclusive Harrogate summer season, when the town was crowded with wealthy visitors. Antonio died in 1859, but his son Antonio carried on the business, moving to no. 2 Crown Place in about 1875, opposite the busy Royal Pump Room. When Harrogate became a borough in 1884, Fattorini's supplied the Mayoral Chain, and again moved premises to their present site at 10 Parliament Street. The business is still run by descendants of Antonio Fattorini, the Tindall family.

Seven
Town's Business

The Pinfold was a device to contain cattle which had strayed, and was provided for the convenience of the Pinder, who was responsible to the Township for such matters. The Harrogate Pinfold was situated at the corner of what is now King's Road and Dawson Terrace.

The Harrogate Electric Lighting Order of 1891 enabled the Harrogate Electricity Undertaking to open a supply on 14 April 1897. Under the care of George Wilkinson, Borough Electrical Engineer from 1897–1927, the area of operations spread throughout the area, taking in Knaresborough in 1924, and Ripon, in 1929. The generating station was situated at Oakdale, where this photograph of the staff was taken, shortly after its opening. In 1936, the undertaking was able to service the first electric crematorium in Britain, which was established in Harrogate.

The Harrogate Electricity showrooms were located in these cottage premises, photographed in 1930, at the corner of Parliament Street and the ginnel footpath. Harrogate Corporation ran not only a municipal electricity undertaking, but also a gas and a telephone service – and ran them successfully. All of these valuable public utilities were overshadowed by the Harrogate Water undertaking, which was on a truly enormous scale. The cottages were demolished in the 1960's to make way for the concrete tower of Harrogate House.

Harrogate Township resolved to obtain a Fire Engine on 31 March 1836 – or rather to contribute 'one fifth of the cost of a fire engine to be paid out of the Parish Rate and that application be made to the various Fire Insurance Offices for their contribution and that the deficiency if any be made up by private subscription'. The outcome is not known, but on 5 November 1855, Richard Ellis reported to the Improvement Commissioners for Harrogate that prices for Fire Engines had been obtained. The Commissioners resolved to spend not more than £120 on such a device. The Harrogate Fire Engine was thus acquired, and promptly forgotten. In 1861 it was reported to be in disrepair, and when Ellis asked for a further report in 1863 he was told that it had been lost! In 1872 complaints revealed that the engine and pump had been removed for other purposes, and finally, in 1873, the surveyor was able to assure the commissioners that the engine was re-assembled and in repair – but now they were without a horse! When the horse was found, it proved to have only one good eye. Ellis despaired. Eventually, however, all was made well, and as proof, the Harrogate Fire Brigade were photographed in 1880. The team, from left to right, were: W. Bungay, G. Shepherd, W. Barker, C. Scholes, G. Wainwright, Watson Gibbon, and Wareham Harry (Harrogate's first Borough Surveyor).

As Harrogate approached the twentieth century, it was realised that the successful future growth of the town would depend on the provision of adequate supplies of pure drinking water. A series of gigantic constructions were planned, under the control of the dynamic Alderman Charles Fortune. In May 1898 the existing Waterworks company was transferred to Harrogate Corporation, and on the following 17 October Alderman Fortune cut the first sod of the Scargill reservoir scheme. An even greater development began in 1903, when the Roundhill reservoir at Haverah Park was begun. It was thanks to these splendid examples of municipal enterprise that Harrogate had ample supplies of drinking water even in years of drought. When some eighty years later Harrogate's water assets were forcibly disposed to the private sector by government decree, the town was robbed on one of the greatest fruits of nineteenth-century public spirit. Here, Alderman Fortune cuts the first sod at Roundhill.

The peak of Harlow Hill lies some 600 feet above sea level. William Grainge, in his history of Harrogate published in 1871, claimed that from here it was possible to see twenty market towns, seventeen castles, twenty-three abbeys and religious houses, over seventy gentlemen's seats, and nearly two hundred churches. The observation tower was built in 1829. A stone carries the names of Alderman David Simpson, Mayor; Edward Wilson Dixon, Engineer; and the Chairman of the Water Board, Alderman Charles Fortune.

Henry Hare's plans for a vast 'Municipal Palace' at the corner of Station Parade and Victoria Avenue. Only the section on the extreme left of the Victoria Avenue wing was ever built, as the town's public library. The Victoria Avenue setting was considered an ideal site to which to transfer the Municipal bureaucracy, as Crescent Gardens was judged too valuable to remain in the unprofitable hands of the Councillors and their officials.

Alderman Fortune was a keen supporter of the Public Library movement, and it was largely at his instigation that Harrogate adopted the Public Libraries Acts in 1886. The first library was established at Fern Villa in Prince's Street in 1887, and this was superseded by a temporary building on the 'Town Hall site' in Victoria Avenue. Thanks to the generosity of Andrew Carnegie (and the urgings of Alderman Fortune!) it was possible to ensure that the first section of the enormous 'Municipal Palace' planned for the corner of Station Parade and Victoria Avenue would contain the Public Library. And thus it was that a distinguished gathering took place on the steps of the newly opened library on 24 January 1906, including: (from left to right) the Town Clerk, J. Turner Taylor; the Mayor, Alderman Neville Williams; the Macebearer, Mr. Fortune; Dr. Kennion, the Bishop of Bath and Wells; and, with watch-chain across his waist-coat, Alderman Charles Fortune, who was doubtless musing of further schemes for the advancement of Harrogate.

Harrogate's Public Library was provided with an Art Gallery in 1930, seen here under construction in the winter of 1929.

The Harrogate Improvement Commissioners gathered in Cambridge Street on 28 February 1874 to lay the foundation stone of the town's first market building, designed by Arthur Hiscoe, who may be seen at extreme left on the front row. This unique record shows all the great men of Victorian Harrogate, save for Dr. Kennion, who had died five and a half years previously, Charles Fortune (who was too young), and Samson Fox (who was still living in Leeds). Those shown are, from left to right: (back row) James Simpson, Richard Hodgson, George Dawson, John Greenwood, William Taylor, Moses Perkin, Richard Ellis, Isaac Thomas Shutt, Charlesworth Thornton, and Malcolm Bateson, Clerk to the Commissioners. On the front row stand Arthur Hiscoe, James Briggs, John Fletcher, James Lomas, John Boddy, James Simpson senior, Henry Greensmith, Samuel Sugden, John Barber (a great promoter of the market, and proprietor of the George Hotel), Revd L. Foote, John Richardson, Dr. Titus DeVille. Harrogate's debt to these men is too great to be calculated.

Harrogate's new Market Hall was opened by the Chairman of the Improvement Commissioners, Henry Greensmith, on 29 August 1874. The building had a principal elevation towards Beulah Terrace (later known as Station Square) with a great clock tower at the junction with Cambridge Street. The clock was a gift from Charles Dickens' great friend the philanthropist Angela Burdett-Coutts, who retained an affection for the town resulting from childhood visits. The large building at right still stands on the junction with Beulah Street, although its ground floor façade has subsequently been replaced with plate glass windows.

Hiscoe's Market Building of 1874 survived a serious fire on 21 March 1914, but the conflagration of 31 January 1937 caused its utter destruction – apart from the tower. Here, the Harrogate Fire Brigade dampen down the still smouldering ruin from a position in Station Square.

The Market Hall shortly after the fire of 1937, showing the intact tower which could easily have been retained. At this time, however, appreciation of Victorian architecture was minimal, and the Borough Architect Leonard Clarke ran up a replacement building within two years. This view in Cambridge Street takes in two cinemas, the St. James, at right with a suspended street canopy, and the Scala 'Super Cinema' opposite, which was built at the far end of Cambridge Street in 1920.

The Harrogate Police Force outside their Raglan Street station. Inspector Gunn stands at left, and Sergt. Butterworth at right. These men kept the streets of Harrogate safe for residents and visitors alike, backed by sensible, summary, and cheap methods of dealing with offenders – especially of the juvenile variety.

Eight

Parks and Gardens

In his *History and Topography of Harrogate* published in 1871, William Grainge described Birk Crag thus: ' … a piece of genuine mountain scenery, consisting of a narrow valley or glen, about half a mile in length, through which run the waters of Oakbeck. The southern side is steep, rugged, and, in some places, precipitous; grey crags peer out of its sides the whole length, but it is only for about two hundred yards in the highest part that they assume their proper majesty – grim and lofty, covered with lichens, the growth of centuries, and perched in such a random manner on the edge of the hill, that apparently a slight force would send them crashing to the bottom …. Here we have nature in her primitive form – man has done nothing to mend or mar her originality, except to delve a paltry stone quarry, thereby displaying his lack of judgement and want of taste. This is the grandest piece of scenery in the neighbourhood of Harrogate; and great is the surprise of the stranger looking down from the top of the Crag to see such a scene in such a situation.' These two Edwardian ladies are seen at Birk Crag shortly before it was bought by three Harrogate councillors for £8,500 with the express intention of keeping it for Harrogate until such time as the Council were willing to buy it for the public. This eventually occurred, thanks to that most public-spirited action.

Crescent Gardens, named after the Crescent Inn which was demolished in the 1890's, became an important centre for Spa promenading during the years before the First World War. Here, we see the gardens during an early morning in the season of 1911. The water cart has already passed, cleansing the streets and dampening any dust so that the ladies' gowns will not be spotted. The visitors have consumed their prescribed doses of Mineral Water at the Royal Pump Room, and now undertake the light exercise of walking around Crescent Gardens.

High Society taking the early morning constitutional in Crescent Gardens during the season of 1911, at the height of the golden age of the Harrogate Spa. The visitors of that year included Queen Alexandra, Prince Henry of Prussia (the Kaiser's brother), Queen Amelia and King Manuel of Portugal, Prince Christopher of Greece, many members of the Imperial British Cabinet, and the regular smattering of Archdukes and Maharajas. The standards of service provided in Harrogate at this time were at almost unprecedented levels, which earned for the town the nickname of 'Heavenly Harrogate'. As these members of fashionable society stroll through an immaculately manicured Crescent Gardens, meeting friends, and enjoying the latest music from the band, they could never have realised that this world was on the brink of Armageddon.

The proximity of Crescent Gardens to the Royal Pump Room, and its central position, meant that it was a popular rendezvous for early morning water drinkers. Vehicular traffic was excluded from the area by means of cordons, with only pedestrian traffic permitted. Thus it was that the heart of Low Harrogate became a 'drawing room', in which smart dress and impeccable behaviour were *de rigueur*. The newly erected shelter stands at left, with the bandstand at centre, and in the background the façades of the George Hotel, the Kursaal and the Spa Rooms. The bandstand had originally stood behind the Montpellier Baths, but was removed when the Royal Baths building was erected on the site.

Opposite (bottom picture): The glorious Rose Gardens behind the Spa Rooms and Kursaal ran the length of King's Road, and were a popular resort for residents and visitors alike. On fine summer evenings they were opened for the pleasure of audiences at the Kursaal, and guests at the Majestic could also take the well-wooded walk which led to pergola path and the roses.

The Rose Gardens, seen here shortly before the First World War, were a development of the gardens of the Spa Rooms which had originally been laid out in 1835. These gardens were part of a much larger estate which lay between the rear of the Kursaal and Spa Rooms, King's Road, and the grounds of the Hotel Majestic. Here could be found the skating rink, tennis courts, and at the eastern extremity, a copse rich in wildlife. This view is from the former Spa Hotel at the junction of the King's Road and Cheltenham Crescent, and includes the Hotel Majestic with its huge conservatory, and the splendid new railings to the Rose Gardens which were the gift to the town of Mr. W.H. Baxter, to commemorate the late King Edward VII and the new King George V. At centre may also be seen the 'orchestra', which was a specially built 'acoustic stand' for musicians, and which became a very popular feature of the town's musical life, especially during the dark days of the First World War. In 1958 the Council decided to experiment with the construction of the town's first purpose-built exhibition hall on the site of the Rose Gardens. The success of the venture in commercial terms resulted in the entire site being filled which exhibition and conference buildings by 1981, by which time the Rose Gardens had become only a memory.

The Valley Gardens came into existence because of a public right of way which ran from the old Sulphur Well to the Bogs Field, crossing land held by the Vicar of Pannal. Bogs Field has always been part of the Harrogate Stray, being part of the Award of 1778, and a much-frequented locale, thanks to the world famous mineral springs which break surface here. Various attempts to embellish the footpath occurred in the nineteenth century, which resulted in the creation of the Valley Gardens. The above photograph was taken *c.* 1917, and shows part of the former Collins Field, which had been purchased by the Council on 15 April 1901 for the express purpose of adding it to the Valley Gardens. Ten years later, the field was still separated from the Valley gardens by a substantial stone wall, despite public grumbling at the Council's tardiness. However, on the night of 13 February 1911 Councillor Binns, the Chairman of the Valley Gardens Committee, led a group of workmen to the offending structure and totally demolished it, thus ensuring the gratitude of generations of visitors, and also an unholy row with his Council colleagues!

This post card view of the Valley Gardens tea house (which stood on the precise site of the later Sun Pavilion) is dated 1917, but was probably taken shortly before the First World War. The text, from a girl to her friend in York, reads: 'We all have been to Birk Crag this afternoon. It is beautiful there, and every morning Pat & I go up on the moors and Pine Woods. I shall miss the lovely and clear air when I come back to York. The shops here are very fascinating – (some swank!). Kindest regards.' The Grand Hotel of 1902 may be seen in the background.

The children's corner of Valley Gardens, photographed in September 1928, showing at centre the old Bandstand and at far right, the Magnesia Well Pump Room. Both buildings were erected in 1895, but the children's pool dates from only the mid-1920's.

Another view of the children's boating pool taken in September 1928 – which has subsequently become a delightful study in period costume.

Thought had been given to the possibility of providing visitors to the Bogs Field with a sheltered promenade as long ago as the 1860's, when Richard Ellis had supported a scheme of improvement. It was not however until the 1920's that the Council began to plan seriously, prompted in part by the need to upgrade facilities for visitors in the light of declining attendance at Spas nationally. A three-part plan was adopted by which the Royal Pump Room would be linked to the Royal Bath Hospital by means of an elegant covered promenade through the beautiful Valley Gardens. A new Pump Room would be built at the Valley Gardens entrance, followed by a pair of 'Sun Parlours', and a glass-domed Sun Pavilion for concerts and light refreshments. Stage one was complete by 1933, and was opened on 17 June by Lord Horder; it included a covered promenade from the site of the proposed new Pump Room, the two 'Sun Parlours', and the splendid Sun Pavilion. The two other stages of the plan were never achieved, as the Council adopted an alternative scheme of improvements at the Royal Baths.

These workers in Sheepshanks Field pause for refreshment during a fine summer day c. 1900. In the background rises the tower of the Baptist Church, and the houses of North Park Road. The splendid curving terrace of East Parade is just off-picture to the right. Sheepshanks Fields disappeared during the inter-war years, when Arthington estate was developed, contrary to Richard Ellis' preferred vision of retaining an open area for leisure purposes which would be different from the Stray. East Parade and Park View were backdrops to the 'park', but the other terraces were never built.

Opposite (bottom picture): The interior of the Sun Pavilion, shortly after its opening on 17 June 1933, showing part of the central seating area and its beautiful stained glass dome. In the centre distance may be seen the cafe, which boasted a trellis suspended from the glass ceiling, along which grew creeping plants. The southern perimeter of the Pavilion was formed with moveable glazed partitions, which were swung back in fine weather to admit the fresh and flower-scented air of the Valley Gardens. The gardens' sparrows also appeared at the tables of the café, being either a source of delight or annoyance according to the visitor's temperament. So long as the Sun Pavilion was the venue for well-planned and attractive entertainments, and the café provided a high standard of service, both were well patronized. During the 1960's and 1970's, the former became less well maintained, and the latter sank to abysmal levels, with the abolition of waitress service, the introduction of cheap plastic utensils, poor refreshments, and an overall air of shabbiness. Eventually it became necessary to close the whole structure on grounds of safety. When the town grew alarmed, it was nearly too late to save the structure. An effort was made, however, and the verandah of the Pavilion was refurbished in 1933, without the glazed partitions or café. At the time of writing, the beautiful pavilion is sealed, awaiting refurbishment for a new lease of life.

STATION PARADE, HARROGATE

The so-called 'Library Gardens' is in fact the site for Harrogate's unfinished 'Municipal Palace', the purpose of which was to provide accommodation for the town's bureaucracy away from the commercially valuable land in Crescent Gardens. One year after Harrogate was Incorporated as a Borough in 1884, the Carter brothers who owned the land were offered £5,000 for the 4,000 square yards at the corner of Station Parade and Victoria Avenue, by a private developer. The offer was rejected, as the site had been ear-marked for the future town hall. Instead, the Carters offered it to Harrogate for only £2,500 on the understanding that it would one day be the site for a Town Hall commensurate with the town's dignity as the World's Greatest Spa. The generous offer was accepted, after being moved by the Mayor, Richard Ellis. After securing an offer from the Carnegie Trust to assist in the provision of a library, work began on 17 October 1904 with the laying of the foundation stone. After completion of the first stage – the library – in 1906, no further work was done and the site was converted into a public garden after the First World War. This, in turn, ensured that the intentions of the designers of the Victoria Park to provide a pleasant town-centre oasis in Princes Square, framed by the imposing architecture and within convenient access of fashionable James Street, was destroyed. As these words are being written, the 'Library Gardens' are famed by the ugly loading bay of the former Co-op building, two traffic-choked highways, and the crude fire-wall of the unfinished Municipal Palace, whereas Princes Square has degenerated into a dumping ground for the polluting presence of the motor car.

Nine
Entertainment

The Harrogate Fife band at the junction of Chapel (now Oxford) Street and Parliament Street, *c.* 1860. At that time, the premises in the background were occupied by the Holroyd photographic studio. Note the paviours which enabled pedestrians to cross the unmade and often muddy surface of both streets.

The pleasant habit of providing live music over the Christmas season developed in Harrogate during the later years of Victoria's reign. The 'Harrogate Waits' shown here are from the season of 1889, their performances having commenced on 4 December of that year.

Visitors to Harlow Moor were provided with musical recitals from a specially constructed band stand, during Edwardian high summers. At left, the Grand Hotel of 1903 may be seen on the horizon, and at right, the houses of Valley Drive. Brass bands and minstrels were the most popular attractions.

This most unusual photograph taken *c.* 1874 shows the gardens of the Montpellier Baths next to the Crown Hotel. When the whole estate was purchased by George Dawson in 1869, a number of improvements were immediately set in hand, including a new Pump Room and a bandstand, seen here at centre. The ginnel is on the far right, just out of picture, and the buildings in the background are part of Bath Terrace, a fine row of Georgian Houses which were demolished in 1954 to make way for the Lounge Hall Car Park. The bandstand was the first to be erected in Harrogate, and did sterling service throughout the 1870's and 1880's. Sidney Jones senior and his band were regular performers here, starting to play at 7.30am, in all weathers! When the Royal Baths were built on the site, the bandstand was removed to Crescent Gardens.

Of all the groups of musicians who performed in the streets and parks of Harrogate, none received such consistently high praise as Otto Schwartz and his Bavarian String Band. Here, they may be seen posing in the Bogs Field at Valley Gardens, in the summer of 1908. Their other regular 'pitch' was Pier Head at the top of Montpellier Hill.

HARROGATE . ROYAL GARDENS . MATINÉE CONCERT . 768

Recitals by Military bands in the gardens of the Spa Rooms were a popular diversion during the terrible years of the Great War, and they continued to draw crowds during the early 1920's. This recital dates from the summer of 1919, the first such summer of the post-war period.

Another very popular troupe of entertainers to appear on Harrogate Stray were the 'Royal Sparks', photographed here in 1909. The message on the back of the post card reads, 'Dear Elsie, this is a troupe on the Stray and their performance is extra. This is how they are dressed – you should see the crowds here. The others can't hold a candle to them'.

Another age, another show. The Revellers appeared in the Valley Gardens in the 1920s, always to the great enthusiasm of the crowds.

When the old High Harrogate theatre of 1788 closed in 1830, the town was without a regular venue for theatrical performances, other than the busy Spa Rooms. Then, in 1882, the Harrogate Amateur Minstrels set up a theatre in the old Town Hall, which became known as the Town Hall Theatre. This venture proved such a success, that plans were drawn up in the 1890s for a new purpose-built theatre, the Opera House. The Old Town Hall Theatre took over the 1805 building of the former Assembly Rooms, which is now the Mercer Art Gallery.

At the height of the celebrations for Queen Victoria's Golden Jubilee in 1887, the people of Harrogate were given the opportunity to view an 'Empire tableau' in the Old Town Hall Theatre, in which leading members of the community represented British possessions and peoples throughout the globe.

Harrogate is most fortunate in that all the buildings of its most important theatres have survived the ravages of time and developers – albeit in modified forms. The Empire Music Hall Theatre, seen here after the First World War, was opened on 22 February 1911 in premises which were adapted from the Primitive Methodist Chapel of 1871–2, designed by Arthur Hiscoe. The man behind the establishment of the Empire was Holden, the puppeteer, whose hands were insured for the phenomenal sum of £5,000. Many famous Music Hall stars appeared on the Empire's stage, which boasted a magnificent proscenium arch – the work of Holden himself. After the Music Hall closed 10 October 1931 Empire Buildings was partly converted into commercial premises, but the auditorium and stage fell into decay. It was subsequently rescued by Fridel Dalling-Hay, who recognised its importance as a monument of old Harrogate. Following a full and skilful restoration of the auditorium and stage in 1986–7, the former Empire Theatre was incorporated with the popular Pinocchio's Restaurant, and rapidly became one of the sights of the town. Tragedy struck in the early hours of Friday 16 September 1994, when an act of criminal arson nearly destroyed Empire Buildings, which were saved thanks to the heroic efforts of the Fire Brigade. The indomitable determination of restaurateur Tony Peral and his staff ensured that Pinocchio's survived the necessary period of closure, rebuilt on a scale more magnificent than before, and re-opened in time for the 1994 Christmas season. Pinocchio's Italian Restaurant in its Empire Buildings location is one of Harrogate's best attractions which should be experienced by all visitors. The restored proscenium arch merits particular attention.

The Grand Opera House opened on 13 January 1900 with a charity performance arranged for *The Gentlemen in Khaki*. A venture of a private company, the building was designed by F.A. Tugwell and has a beautiful interior with rich plasterwork. The Art Nouveau frieze in the entrance hall is an unusual and interesting feature worthy of inspection. Another unusual and thoroughly inconvenient feature is the fact that all of all the theatres known to the author, this is the only one to close down an existing cloakroom, requiring the audience to either sit in wet coats, or place them on the floor. The external canopy was a useful feature, as it afforded protection to pedestrians. At far right may be seen the trees of Cheltenham Parade, which in 1900 was a pleasant residential area.

The interior of the 'Grand Opera House' shortly after its opening in 1900. The theatre then had a seating capacity of 1,300.

The Harrogate Cycling Club put on a splendid procession as part of the town's festivities for the Coronation of Edward VII in 1902. Here, one of the cyclists may be seen going the wrong way round Victoria Circus, with the Claremont Hotel, and a heavily-tree'd residents' 'pleasure garden' in the background.

Tom Coleman and his pierrots were one of the best-loved of the several bands of performers who entertained the crowds in pre-First World War Harrogate. Although it was said somewhat uncharitably that his songs verged, occasionally, on the saucy, this does not appear to have worried the crowds who gathered to listen. Here, Tom Coleman performs from his regular pitch on Bogs Field in Valley Gardens, during the summer of 1910. The Royal Bath Hospital is in the background.

Edmund Candler's 'Permanent Punch and Judy Show' appears to have been established at some point in the early 1860s. Its site in front of the White Hart Hotel in Low Harrogate proved especially popular with those visitors who arrived in the town by coach. At right, the photographer has captured a moment which has given the gathered children particular delight. Edmund Candler's father appears to have had a Marionette show in Harrogate c. 1814, but details have not survived.

This Harrogate street musician has pitched his cart in the developing Dragon estate in the early years of the twentieth century. Two boys, who could have stepped from the pages of A.A. Thomson's novel about old Harrogate, *The Exquisite Burden*, appear to be the only audience.

Although 'animated films' had been shown in the St James's Hall in Cambridge Street as early as 1907, Harrogate had to wait until 1920 for its first purpose-built 'super cinema', when the Scala (later Gaumont) opened. The Scala was built on land which had formerly housed the stables for the Prospect Hotel. When the cinema closed in 1959, it was replaced in 1962 by Littlewoods store.

Ten

Spa Rooms and Kursaal

The Kursaal Tea Room, Harrogate.

The former 'long gallery' of 1871 was converted for use as a café for the Kursaal, following the completion of that building in 1903. This photograph is taken from a contemporary postcard, and shows at right the south-facing wall of the Kursaal, and at left the newly-formed opening into the north wall of the 1835 Spa Rooms. With its elegant palms and resident musicians, the Kursaal Café was the most fashionable in Harrogate before the First World War. At night it served as an invaluable overflow for both the Kursaal and Spa Rooms. The destruction of the 'long gallery' and the Spa Rooms in 1939 was the worst architectural blunder ever to be committed in Harrogate.

The Kursaal opened on 28 May 1903, and thereafter the world's greatest artistic talents appeared on its stage. Throughout the golden years of Edwardian Harrogate, names of the calibre of Busoni, Elgar, Kreisler and Melba drew capacity audiences, and the management planned programmes to cater to the widest possible range of tastes. The Kursaal is a unique surviving example of a type of building which barely exists today, being a true Kursaal with a floor which was level, rather than raked, and a series of encircling promenades in keeping with the requirements of Spa fashion. The photograph shows an audience departing from a matinee, at which Dan Leno was the star attraction. Two points of architectural interest – the bowl-structure on the cornice at left was a gas-powered flambeau which produced a dramatic torch of flame when switched on at night – above the central tympanum of the glazed entrance canopy rides a cockerel, not as a weathervane, but as a symbol of healing, taken from the Greek god Asklepios, god of medicine and healing, to whom it was usual to sacrifice a cock as thanks for recovery from illness.

Opposite (bottom picture): The Mineral Waters from the Spa Rooms estate were served in the new Pump Room after its opening in 1871, and the older building of the Spa Rooms was reserved purely for leisure and entertainment. An interesting feature of the new pump room was a bust of the internationally celebrated chemist, Dr. Muspratt, who had carried out a thorough analysis of the waters in 1868. The importance of Dr. Muspratt was such that his enthusiastic endorsement of the Harrogate Wells encouraged a considerable increase in the numbers of patients resorting to the Spa for cures. It was no less a personage than Charles Dickens who suggested that Harrogate should honour Muspratt's work by erecting 'a marble bust to Dr. Maspratt ... beneath some stately pump room.'

Harrogate Corporation acquired the Spa Rooms estate in 1896, and almost immediately began to consider plans for the construction of a great new building which would provide Harrogate with a hall worthy of the twentieth century – then only four years away. After the invariable disagreements and rows over designs and costs, the plans of R.J. Beale were adopted, which were to be enhanced by the brilliant Frank Matcham, one of the very greatest designers of theatres. The foundation stone was laid by the Mayor, Alderman David Simpson, at 3.00pm on 4 January 1902. The chain which suspended the stone is visible clearly in this photograph. The Mayor and Mace-bearer stand to the immediate right of the chain, overlooked by the be-wigged Town Clerk, Turner-Taylor. To the left of the chain stands the commanding figure of Alderman Charles Fortune, the real driving force behind all of Harrogate's expansive schemes at this period. The Mayor's words were singularly apt: 'No corporation can be successful without the absolute confidence and respect of the inhabitants. Harrogate has always possessed men of spirit, capacity, and energy. My name is registered on the stone, and I would not like to be told in years to come – you were an old fool David Simpson, to lay that stone. However, I believe that future generations will appreciate our efforts today'. The Borough brass band then launched into a rousing rendition of Dr. Elgar's splendid new Imperial March, and amidst cheers from the crowd, the National Anthem was played.

The discovery in 1818 of the Cheltenham Spring in a field at the corner of Ripon Road and the future King's Road, proved to be a valuable addition to Harrogate's supply of Chalybeate (or Iron) Waters, and one which eventually turned out to be the strongest chloride of iron water in Europe. Highly favoured by the medical profession, the Cheltenham Spring attracted many drinkers, and the estate eventually passed into the hands of John Williams, the businessman who developed the Victoria Baths across what later became Crescent Gardens. Williams realised the value of the site, and commissioned Leeds architect Clarke to build him a pump and assembly room which would outstrip in magnificence everything else in Harrogate. The result was the Cheltenham Spa Rooms, which was for long regarded as Harrogate's most perfect building. This photograph of 1910 includes at right a section of the Manager's house, which spoiled the classic simplicity of the south façade, and at left, a section of the glazed extension of 1871, which connected the Spa Rooms to the Kursaal.

Opposite: The 1871 extensions were a brilliant way of enlarging the 1835 Spa Rooms without detracting from the austere classical magnificence of the original structure. The technology of the Crystal Palace was allied to the fanciful architecture of the Brighton Pavilion to produce a unique example of fantastic Spa design, which drew much favourable comment from the visitors. The new structures were illuminated internally at night with many tiny coloured lights, which gave an impression of something from the *Thousand and One Nights*. This photograph of 1871, taken a little after the completion of the annex, shows how the ensemble appeared from Ripon Road.

A joint stock company was formed in 1862 by fifteen Harrogate businessmen for the purpose of purchasing the Cheltenham Spa Rooms, and instituting a major series of improvements. The estate was bought for a little over £5,000, and work began immediately on its improvement. The gardens were re-formed, and embellished with statuary and fountains, and imaginative programmes arranged for the entertainment of visitors – the great Blondin being a particularly popular attraction. Despite these improvements, the company failed to make a profit, but rather than give up the venture, the Board decided to extend the Spa Rooms themselves, and set up a competition, with was won by Bown, the distinguished local architect. Bown's proposal was to add a glazed promenade to the north side of the Spa Rooms, which would provide visitors with means to walk in the worst of weather, and which would also serve as an extension for the grand saloon of the original Spa Rooms. In addition, there was to be a new pump room for the famous Cheltenham Spring, crowned by a soaring dome. This photograph of c. 1880 shows the back of the new glazed promenade and Pump Room, taken from the grounds. The George Hotel may also be seen between the columns of the ornamental band-stand.

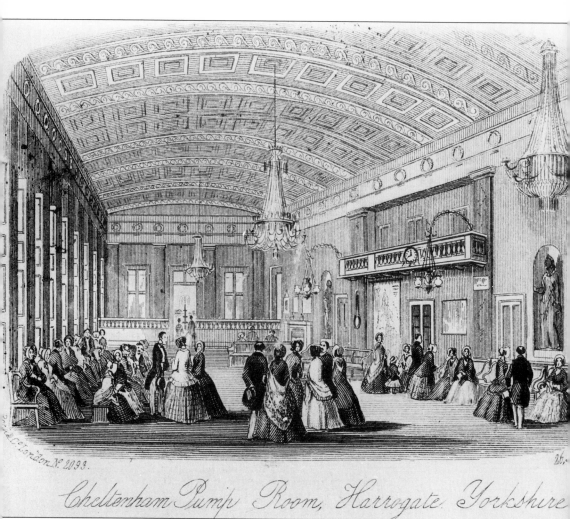

Cheltenham Pump Room, Harrogate Yorkshire

The grand saloon of the Spa Rooms, pictured on 26 June 1860, a quarter of a century after its opening in 1835. The wealth of decoration was restricted to the great vault of the ceiling, from which three enormous chandeliers were suspended. This contrasted with the classical elegance of the walls and floor, which relied on the spare proportions and relations of ranges of pilasters and windows to create an effect. At right may be seen the musicians' gallery from which a chamber ensemble could serenade the visitors. The distant dais contained space for a larger orchestra, as well as a stage for dramatic performances and readings. The door at the very back of the saloon opened into the gardens, which stretched as far as the site of the modern Conference Centre. But for its destruction in 1939, this epitome of Georgian splendour would have been a perfect setting for the many prestigious conference and exhibition assemblies which in later times would become such an important part of Harrogate's economy.

Eleven

Church and Faith

Christ Church was built in 1831 to replace the 1749 Chapel of St. John, as the latter building had become too small. Its location at the heart of High Harrogate made it an obvious site for the memorial erected in honour or Dr. Kennion, whose death in 1868 was mourned by the entire community. This photograph of Christ Church is of interest, as it shows not only the four pinnacles of the tower, which were dismantled in the early years of the twentieth century, but also the 'High Harrogate Ghost', at the foot of the tower. This was the familiar name for the statue commissioned by the town as a memorial to Dr. Kennion. The sculpture took the form of a sixteen-foot-high 'broken column with drapery', set upon a bas-relief portrait of the Doctor. The new work was greeted with universal indignation, as it gave the 'kind hearted man of great talents' a decidedly mean look and a profile with a sinister leer. After a great row, letters between solicitors, and much airing of opinions in the *Advertiser*, the irate Vicar put an end to the affair by ordering the removal of the sculpture in March 1873.

Cheltenham Parade meets Oxford (formerly Chapel) Street at the point where the old Beulah Chapel was erected in 1824. An earlier Chapel for the Methodists had been opened in 1796 at 20 Park Parade (which locals referred to facetiously as 'Paradise Row') but the growing Wesleyans soon required larger accommodation, and the 1824 Chapel was built by David Simpson for £1,011. It lasted until it became too small, and was replaced by the present magnificent Chapel of 1862 which was built further along Chapel Street at the junction with Cheltenham Crescent. The 1824 Chapel was then sold and converted into retail property, seen here c. 1905.

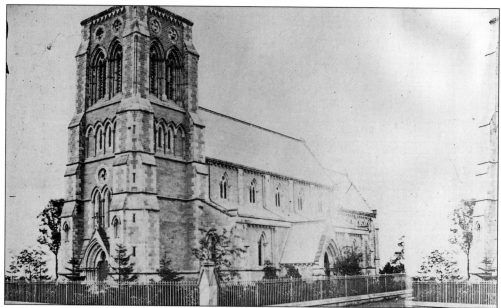

Sir George Gilbert Scott intended his great church of St. John at Bilton to be surmounted with a soaring spire, to off-set the massive tower at the west front. St. John's was built from 1851–7, and was more fortunate that St. Mark's Church, built fifty years later, in that the tower was completed. Unfortunately, however, the spire remains unbuilt, although the advent of Heritage funds from the National Lottery may one day give somebody an idea. St. John's is in the Early English style of architecture, and has a nave of five bays, and some fine internal decoration, including stained glass by Grace, and a great open timber roof with trefoil trusses.

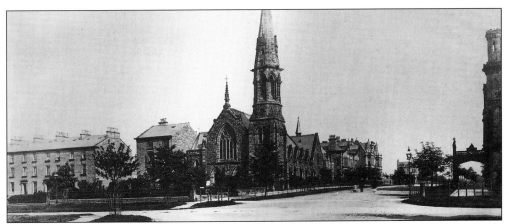

From the point of overall townscape importance, few of Harrogate's churches occupy so significant a position as the Congregational Chapel (United Reformed Methodist) built in 1861–2 by Lockwood and Mawson at the junction of West Park with the brand new Victoria Avenue. Victoria Avenue was the show-street of the Victoria Park Company's great development of the open fields between the two ancient villages of High and Low Harrogate. This photograph of *c.* 1880 shows the Church in relation to the Belvedere building opposite, and the private residences of West Park. At this time, Victoria Avenue was a private thoroughfare, and the footpaths were provided with railings and gateways for the use of residents. The Belvedere was built in 1861 as a private mansion for the banker J. Smith of Burley.

The Victoria Park Methodist Church was built in Station Parade in 1865 by Richard Ellis, to a design by J.H. Hirst. The building of this church was a project dear to Ellis's heart, as it not only provided the Victoria Park Company (of which Ellis was a principal director and resident) with a fine Methodist Church, but was a suitable neighbour for the long-planned Town Hall, intended for the adjoining site at the corner of Victoria Avenue. The Church was endowed generously by Ellis. After being declared redundant after the Second World War, it was acquired by the Co-operative Society, demolished in 1953, and replaced by a cretinous shoe-box of a building.

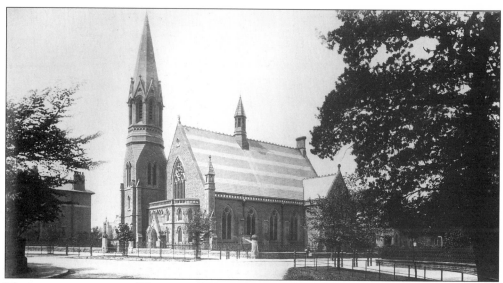

The young community of Harrogate Baptists first submitted plans for a chapel in 1877, but as they under-estimated the demand for capacity, it became necessary to submit revised proposals in February 1882, and the present building was erected in 1883. The church, with its nave of four bays, transept, tower and spire, is a fine example of Victorian Gothic, and is favoured with an excellent site in Victoria Avenue overlooking Victoria Circus. This photograph shows the Church shortly after completion. At left may be seen part of the circus boundary, which encircled a pleasure garden for the residents of the Victoria Park estate. A bandstand was built here in 1895, at which Sidney Jones would often perform with his band.

The men who built St. Luke's Church, posing for the photographer before their handiwork. After a 'mission hall' had been opened at Smithy Hall, Skipton Road, in 1888, it had become obvious that there was a need for a new Parish Church to be provided for the locality. An anonymous gift of £1,000 started a fund for the new church, but a controversy began when the Vicar of Christ Church, the Revd R.W. Fawkes, announced that he had had an offer of an endowment for the living, on condition that the patronage was granted to the donor. On the other hand, Baron De Ferriers, who owned most of the land in the neighbourhood, offered to make a gift of what is now the site on condition that the patronage of the living went to the Bishop. The Baron's offer was eventually and gratefully accepted, and the new Church of St. Luke was built in 1897. Consecration was by the Bishop of Ripon, Dr. W. Boyd-Carpenter, on 18 October 1897. St. Luke's Church became redundant in 1979 but was converted into 29 small flats in 1984, although its massive exterior appears little altered.

Opposite: A chapel for the Wesleyan Methodists of Starbeck was erected in The Avenue in 1888–9, having accommodation for 200 people, and a school for 60 children. The chapel served until 1929, when the Wesleyan and Primitive Methodists decided to amalgamate. A new chapel was then built in 1930–1, and the old chapel eventually became Starbeck Library.

The Citadel of the Salvation Army, built next to the former Methodist Chapel at the corner of Beulah Street, Chapel Street, and Station Parade, is seen in this photograph of c. 1925. The building contains an impressive hall, and the large windows, mansard roof, and dramatic skyline make it an important addition to the architecture of the area. At far left may be seen the cottages for the workers of the North Eastern Railway. At this time, Station Parade and Cheltenham Parade were both quiet, tree-lined residential areas.

St. Mark's Church was built in Leeds Road in 1904 to serve the residential developments which had sprung into being in the late Victorian era. Designed by J. Oldrid Scott, St. Mark's Church was originally intended to have an imposing tower, but this was never constructed. For many years the west front remained in an incomplete condition, until plans for a rose window and two small towers were drawn up by F.L. Charlton after the Second World War. St. Mark's Church was consecrated on 29 July 1905 by the Bishop of Ripon, Dr. Boyd-Carpenter, and its first Vicar was the Revd W.Y. Potter. The Parish was carved from those of Pannal, St. Peter's and St. Mary's.

Twelve
Education

The long-vanished school buildings of the former 'Strawberry Dale Academy' at the corner of Mayfield Grove and Strawberry Dale, *c*. 1900. This was Low Harrogate's principal place of primary education before the opening of the British School in Chapel Street in 1835, and before the Church Schools of St. Mary's and St. Peter's were built.

Church Square, High Harrogate, photographed *c.* 1860 from the south. The cottages partly obscure the front of the school which was established here in 1837, largely thanks to the efforts of William Sheepshanks, and the Duchy of Lancaster. The school became High Harrogate's principal place of education, with generations of the town's children passing through its doors (including the author of this book!). As a church school, it had close links with neighbouring Christ Church. When the school merged with St. Aidan's School, the old buildings were used for other educational purposes, before being demolished in 1987 to make way for a beautiful housing development which was fully in harmony with the rest of historic Church Square.

St. Mary's School, located conveniently near to old St. Mary's Church, was established in 1837 thanks to a generous grant from the Duchy of Lancaster. The building shown here was built in 1851, and after becoming redundant, it was used for the Y.M.C.A. and for the Jewish Community's Synagogue, which was opened by the Chief Rabbi, Dr. J.H. Hertz, on 9 September 1925. Eventually, the building was demolished and replaced by a new Synagogue in 1968. At left may be seen the rear premises of Beech Lodge and Beech Villa.

A bird's eye representation of the Western College, at the corner of Cold Bath Road and Queen's Road, drawn in the late nineteenth century. All of the buildings survive, having been modified for residential use after the removal of the school, c. 1914.

The buildings of the former Harrogate Technical School on Haywra Crescent were, together with the neighbouring Dragon Road Methodist Church, the most splendid public buildings on the Dragon estate. Both were destroyed in the second half of the twentieth century.

Harrogate Ladies' College moved from Dirlton Lodge on Ripon Road to new premises in the Oval. The college, a famous Harrogate institution, attracts pupils from all over the world to its Clarence Drive buildings.

The children of Oatlands Mount Council School posed for the photographer in the summer of 1908, under the watchful eyes of their Headmaster, Mr. T. Wilde, at right, and Miss Arnold, at left.

The foundation stone for a great new school for girls was laid on 21 October 1909, work being completed by 27 September 1912. The ceremonial opening was performed by the Duchess of St. Albans, who arrived at Harrogate Railway Station to be greeted by the Mayor, Councillor Rowntree (at left), members of the Council, and the Town Clerk, J. Turner Taylor (second from left). The demolition of the buildings of Queen Ethelburga's in 1995, after the school had moved to Thorpe Underwood, was regretted by many of the town's people, who regarded the old red brick structure with affection.

132

Thirteen
Celebrations

To commemorate Queen Victoria's Golden Jubilee in 1887, the Mayor of Harrogate, Alderman Richard Ellis, presented the town with a statue of the Queen, together with a splendid Gothic canopy. The monument was designed by H.E. & A. Bown, and the statue was sculpted by Webber of London. When the foundation stone was laid by the Mayoress, Mrs. Ellis, Station Square was little more than a random collection of utilitarian buildings and an uncultivated open space in front of the Railway Station. James Street, however, was the formal entrance to Harrogate, along which passed the carriages of newly-arrived visitors. The statue of the Queen was accordingly placed to overlook the route. This photograph shows the crowds gathering round the Mayoress on 23 June 1887, as the stone is laid. The Railway Station may be seen in the background, shortly before the glazed canopy was erected over the forecourt.

On 25 June 1887, beneath a blue sky and brilliant sunshine, the festive parade to commemorate the Golden Jubilee of Queen Victoria made its way through the town centre, climbing a Parliament Street festooned with flags and bunting. At left may be seen the lock-up shops built by George Dawson on the Parliament Street boundary of his Crown Hotel estate, which at the time of this photograph was a thickly wooded pleasure garden. Parliament Street was laid out for the needs of the people, rather than vehicles, as the width of the pavements demonstrate.

One of the more spectacular celebrations of Queen Victoria's Golden Jubilee in 1887 was the public Ox Roasting provided by Samson Fox on High Harrogate Stray. Fox was one of the most extraordinary men ever to live in the town, being an inventor and engineer of genius, as well as a brilliant man of business. Two of his inventions achieved worldwide success: the Fox Patent Rolled Steel Corrugated Boiler Flue, and the Fox Patent Pressed Steel Rolling Stock. The latter was introduced with great success to the USA, with the assistance of 'Diamond Jim' Brady. At the 1893 Chicago World Exposition, Samson Fox had the satisfaction of seeing in use the first steel freight cars in America, the product of his Illinois Steelworks. Fox was a splendid Mayor of Harrogate, providing public Ox Roastings on three occasions. Here, Samson Fox, sporting a peaked cap, inspects the ox roasting machinery.

When Queen Victoria's grandson, Prince Albert Victor, visited Harrogate in 1889 to open the enlarged Royal Bath Hospital, the town gave him a splendid reception. Samson Fox donated a couple of impressive arches for the Royal visitor to pass beneath (one on Skipton Road and another on Well Hill), and James Street was turned into a *via triumphalis*. Special care was lavished on the Queen's statue, then only two years old, which boasted magnificent iron railings.

The year 1897 was one of the town's high points. Not only was this the time of Queen Victoria's Diamond Jubilee, but it was the year of the opening of the Royal Baths by H.R.H. The Duke of Cambridge. The opening took place on 3 July, with a tour of the building by the Duke, and a grand assembly in the palm-bedecked Wintergardens, at which a choral concert was provided as accompaniment to the speeches!

The climax of an era – the Golden Jubilee monument decorated for the Diamond Jubilee of the Queen-Empress Victoria, 22 June 1897. At the time this morning photograph was taken, the Queen was making her historic progress through London in similar brilliant sunshine. The temperature in the shade in Harrogate at that time of the town's own procession was 76 degrees The procession was headed by a company of twenty Yorkshire Hussars, and the bells of Harrogate's churches contributed to the occasion. The Duke of Devonshire sent Queen Victoria a special commemorative album bound in Morocco of views of Harrogate and Knaresborough, which included presentation wishes.

The Primitive Methodists' first church was built in 1855 in Westmorland Passage, having a seating capacity of 200. The second, and much more substantial church was built in 1871–2 at the corner of Mount Street and Cheltenham Parade to a design of Arthur Hiscoe's. When this second church became inadequate for the needs of the community, a third church was built at the corner of Bower Road and Dragon Parade, being opened in 1900 on 18 September. Built in the English decorated style of architecture, with a fine tower, the Dragon Parade Methodist Church played an important role in the civic life of the town, as many of its members were civic dignitaries. In this photograph of 1901 the civic party passes the church, with Alderman David Simpson, the Mayor, and Turner-Taylor the Town Clerk. The church closed in 1968, with demolition following shortly afterwards. The site remained empty for nearly twenty-five years, until a residential development was built, the finishing touches of which are being added as these words are set down.

Harrogate put out the flags and bunting in 1902 to mark the coronation of the King-Emperor Edward VII. This view of Parliament Street shows the Gothic tower of the Westminster Arcade, built on the site of Dr. Deville's house in 1897. A man pauses in the middle of the street, apparently to light his pipe, in sublime indifference to any passing vehicular traffic!

Before a vast crowd, the Mayor of Harrogate, Captain A.B. Boyd-Carpenter, proclaims from the steps of the Royal Baths the accession of George V, May 1910. The occasion has been captured by a photographer who has climbed onto the roof of Grosvenor Buildings. From left to right may be seen the George Hotel, the Hotel Majestic, the Kursaal, and the Spa Rooms. In the crowd, the male fashion for straw boaters is clearly evident, and on Ripon Road, motor cars outnumber horse-drawn vehicles.

The crowd awaiting outside the Municipal Offices on 15 December 1936 for proclamation of the accession of King George VI. Part of the elaborate iron and glass bandstand may be seen at extreme left.

King George V, with Queen Mary, arrived at Harrogate Station on 21 August 1933, travelling on the Royal Train. The King is accompanied by Lord Harewood. Queen Mary visited the Harrogate antique shops with regularity.

Harrogate has had a tradition of supporting lifeboat charities since the time of the Carter sisters endeavours. In 1904, the town came to the rescue of the Hartlepool Lifeboat Fund, which culminated with a grand procession through Harrogate, featuring the new lifeboat and its crew. The day of celebration was on Saturday 23 july 1904, the event starting from the Victoria Baths in Crescent Gardens. Headed by the Borough Band, the procession moved up Parliament Street, along 'The Front' (West Park), round the Prince of Wales' corner, York Place, Station Parade, Victoria Avenue, Queen Parade, Park Parade, Regent Parade, Devonshire Place, and finally into the football field grounds. Many floats were included, such as that from the 'Little Wonder Inn' which was a model lifeboat manned by eight boys from Bilton, wearing blue jerseys and cork belts. The St. Peter's Lifeboat float was also admired, as it looked the part, and was filled with children dressed in smocks. To round off the procession, the band of the Harrogate Fire Brigade performed rousing marches. At a tug of war in the ensuing jollities on the football pitch, the Town Clerk, J. Turner-Taylor, was dragged several yards through the mud, to the evident delight of the spectators! The photographer, Mr. Riley Fortune, captured the procession as it passed the Queen Hotel on Park Parade.

The Lord Mayor of London, Sir David Burnett, visited Harrogate to open the annex to the Royal Pump Room on 7 June 1913. The state landau was transported to Harrogate by train, and paraded through the streets to receive a rapturous welcome from the crowds. As guests of the Corporation, the Mayors or Lord Mayors of York, Leeds, Bradford, Barnsley, Beverley, Bridlington, Dewsbury, Doncaster, Halifax, Huddersfield, Hull, Keighley, Middlesborough, Morley, Ossett, Pontefract, Pudsey, Ripon, Todmorden, and Wakefield, had been invited to attend the splendid ceremonies and lavish banquets arranged to commemorate the occasion. After the opening reception at the Queen Hotel in High Harrogate, the procession left for a tour of the town, headed by mounted police and the band of the Yorkshire Hussars. This photograph was taken after the Lord Mayor of London had opened the Royal Pump Room annex and as the state landau was ascending Montpellier Hill.

The extensions to the Royal Baths were opened on 10 July 1939 by Sir Frank Bowater, the Lord Mayor of London, who brought the state landau in which he drove through the streets of Harrogate. The event was watched by crowds of people, some of whom may have recalled the previous visit by a Lord Mayor of London, when Sir David Burnett opened the annex to the Royal Pump Room on 7 June 1913.

The twinning of Harrogate with the French resort of Luchon dates from 1953, when the Mayor of Luchon, Monsieur Alfred Floret, forged the link. French Week, however, was a much broader affair; which was in part the product of a feeling in post-War Britain that it was going to be important to forge friendly links with Europe. During the 1950's and 1960's, French Week, and later, Italian Week, were popular parts of Harrogate's social calendar. These photographs show some of the events for French Week which were mounted in Crescent Gardens, *c*. 1960.

Fourteen

War

The Harrogate Defence League played an important role in raising awareness of the need for military preparedness in the population. Here, the League stands in line in Station Parade, under the shadow of the Victoria Park Methodist Church. Union Jacks fly from the towers of the North Eastern Hotel, and the summer of 1914 is still at its height.

The army's recruiting team arrived in Harrogate shortly after the outbreak of the international catastrophe of 1914. Taking up residence in Westminster Chambers, at the corner of Station Parade and Victoria Avenue, the team toured Harrogate in a series of impressive motor cars, and launched a series of impassioned appeals to the young men of the town.

The Ackrill press photographer was on hand to 'snap' the very first batch of volunteer recruits as they left Westminster Chambers. In common with their counterparts all over Europe, these men prepared for the future with a cheerful countenance and a clear conscience.

The regular recruiting office was established a little later in Raglan Street, and it was through their portals that the majority of the town's recruits passed. 'Lord Derby's Recruiting Office' later became the home of a firm of solicitors. These men were recruits from the post office.

The training undergone by members of the Harrogate Defence League was considered rather fun. Here, the men may be seen at target practice on the miniature range behind the Kursaal – which would soon be renamed the 'Royal Hall'.

The Harrogate Pal's Company and 5th West Yorkshire Volunteers march up Station Parade in 1914 towards the Railway Station. In the background stand the cottages occupied by the railwaymen, which would later be demolished to provide a site for the central Bus Station.

These soldiers, led by Borough Treasurer Stephenson, marched round the town immediately before leaving Harrogate by rail. At the bottom of Parliament Street, they turned into Crescent Gardens …

146

... and marched round the Royal Pump Room, symbol of Harrogate, before climbing Montpellier Hill for the central Station. For many, this was to prove a final farewell.

This group of Harrogate voluntary nurses pose for the camera at the railway station during the Great War.

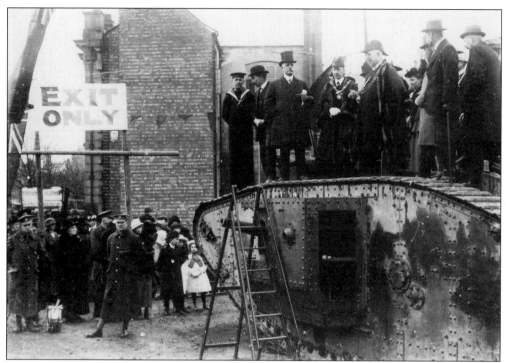

As part of its contribution towards the national war effort, Harrogate raised funds for a tank – which was subsequently known as the 'Harrogate Tank'. Here it is in library gardens, with the Mayor, F.G. Johnson, standing on top of it.

The Russian flag day was supported enthusiastically by the girls of Harrogate, who started their fund raising drive at the office for Belgian refugees in Raglan Street.

The Grand Hotel was converted into the Furness Military Hospital, during the First World War. Consequently, the neighbouring Valley Gardens became a popular meeting place for the Military – and their many female admirers!

During the terrible years of the First World War, the Kursaal (which changed its name to that of the Royal Hall) mounted many entertainments for the wounded soldiers who were recovering in Harrogate. This competition to find the best imitator of Charlie Chaplin was won by Sergeant Hogg, D.C.M., at the extreme right. The stained glass windows of the Kursaal gallery may be seen in the background.

In the early years of the Second World War, Harrogate Corporation established a demonstration house in a property on Well Hill, opposite the Royal Pump Room, to instruct the population in matters of air raid precautions.

The south Stray was planted with corn during the Second World War which at high summer converted a sea of emerald green into one of gold.

The Stray harvest of 1941. The tower of Christ Church rises between the two hay-stacks at left. The footpath is the one which connects Wedderburn House with Wetherby Road.

Harrogate was attacked by a lone German aircraft on 12 September 1940, which had been sent to destroy the Crown and Majestic Hotels. Both buildings had been requisitioned by the Government following the outbreak of the Second World War, and a surviving map produced by the German Air Ministry shows that both hotels were considered military targets. After circling the town, the pilot released his bombs, which fell on an empty house at the corner of Ripon and Swan Roads, on the gardens of the Hotel Majestic, and on the Hotel Majestic itself. The house was demolished, but the one which fell on the Majestic penetrated the building, hit a girder, and rebounded into a fifth-floor bedroom – fortunately it failed to explode. Thanks to the efficiency and bravery of the bomb disposal unit under Captain Yates, the unexploded bomb was de-fused and removed from the hotel. Only a few people had been injured by the attack, including the wife of the hotel's door attendant, Mrs. Kirksopp, who sadly died of her injuries a few days later. Here, the de-fused bomb lies outside the shattered conservatory of the Hotel Majestic.

The villa at the junction of Swan and Ripon Roads was less fortunate than the Hotel Majestic, as the bombs demolished the building completely. It was not rebuilt until 1987, when Goldsborough Healthcare plc erected an attractive replacement structure.

The explosions which demolished the Swan Road villa and shattered the glass of the Hotel Majestic's Conservatory, also wrecked the windows of the shops in King's Road. In this photograph, staff are sweeping up the broken glass.

Several enemy planes came down in the Harrogate area during the Second World War. The remains of one of them were photographed in Duchy Road.

The Prime Minister, Winston Churchill, visited Harrogate in 1944, and was given a friendly but discreet welcome by townspeople gathered at the Railway Station.

The memorial to the dead of two World Wars stands at the centre of the town in Prospect Square, overlooked by the two great crescents created by George Dawson. It was unveiled on 1 September 1923 to commemorate the sons of Harrogate who had perished in the First World War of 1914–1918, and some twenty years later was also dedicated to the memory of the fallen of the Second World War of 1939–1945. The monument, built on land which had once been the pleasure gardens of the Prospect Hotel, is a simple but extremely effective statement, and is seen here *c.* 1950 when the recent sacrifices were still terribly fresh in the town's collective memory.

Fifteen
Sport

A game of Rugby in progress on Harrogate Stray, *c* 1870.

The Harrogate Hunt, outside the Crown Hotel, *c.* 1855. The central portion of the Crown Hotel had been rebuilt in 1847, to a handsome Palladian design, but the older wings had to wait until George Dawson arrived on the scene in 1869. Harrogate was often advertised as being an ideal centre for hunting. When this photograph was taken, open country was only a few minutes' canter away, as Low Harrogate ended beyond Well Hill.

A charity cricket match was held at Harrogate Cricket Club on 8 July 1909 between Clergymen and Doctors.

The Harrogate Men's lacrosse match, West Park Stray, *c.* 1890. The club appears to have been established in 1886.

Harrogate has seldom been associated with water sports, but the last quarter of the nineteenth century witnessed an upsurge of interest in boating, thanks to the provision of a large boating pond on the Spa Rooms estate. On special occasions, the fun went on through the night, and the boats and trees which surrounded the pool were festooned with chinese lanterns. Such boating 'regattas' usually ended with a fireworks display, which the town's Jeremiahs claimed were timed specially to 'waken the invalid and affright the nervous'.

This view could only have been taken in 1901–2, as the Hotel Majestic had been completed in 1900, and the empty boating pool at left was covered in 1902 when work began on the new Kursaal. The boating pool was emptied every winter so that the sport of skating could be enjoyed by residents and visitors alike.

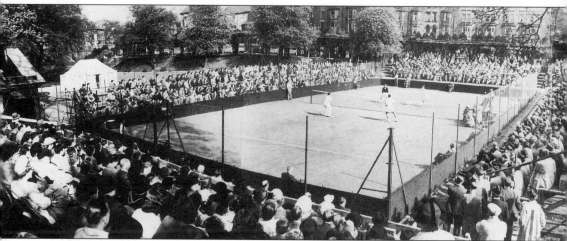

After the Council acquired the Spa Rooms estate in 1896 and built the Kursaal, it was decided to replace the vanished boating pool and rink with a series of tennis courts. The new amenity was constructed to meet the highest standards of international tennis, and the Davis Tournament was subsequently played here in 1926.

Acknowledgements

The author acknowledges with gratitude the co-operation of those businesses who have supplied him with photographs: Betty's, for the photograph on page 75; Fattorini's, for the photograph on page 82; Ogden's, for the photograph on page 73; Wood, for the photograph on page 63. Special thanks are also due to the expert on Harrogate's postal history, Clifford Hopes, whose generosity in allowing the author access to his unrivalled collection of Harrogate post cards has made this book better than it would otherwise have been.

The author had the privilege of interviewing, shortly before her death, Mary Topham, the daughter of Harrogate's great Town Clerk, J. Turner-Taylor. Some of the accounts of events witnessed and the personalities known by Mrs. Topham, have been included in this book.

To all of these donors, the author extends his thanks.